MW01032457

"AARON BANK'S CONTRIBUTIONS TO THE HERITAGE OF SPECIAL FORCES HAVE BEEN UNIQUE. . . . AMERICANS WHO ARE REALLY INTERESTED IN THE EVENTS LEADING UP TO THE DEVELOPMENT OF ONE OF THE MOST EXTRAORDINARY MILITARY ORGANIZATIONS THEIR NATION HAS PRODUCED, CAN FIND NO GREATER AUTHORITY THAN AARON BANK."
—Lt. Gen. William P. Yarborough,
U.S. Army Special Forces (Ret.)

"THE TRUE, TOP-SECRET STORY . . . BY THE MAN WHO MADE IT HAPPEN! THIS BOOK BELONGS ON EVERY MILITARY BOOKSHELF!"
—Capt. Shelby Stanton, U.S. Army (Ret.),
author of *Green Berets at War*

"BENEATH COL. AARON BANK'S FRIENDLY DEMEANOR . . . IS A BACKGROUND OF INTRIGUE, DRAMA AND BLOODSHED . . ."
—*San Clemente Sun-Post*

# FROM OSS TO GREEN BERETS

## BERETS

**The Birth of Special Forces**

## COL. AARON BANK, U.S.A. (RET.)

PUBLISHED BY POCKET BOOKS NEW YORK

POCKET BOOKS, a division of Simon & Schuster, Inc.
1230 Avenue of the Americas, New York, N.Y. 10020

Published by arrangement with Presidio Press
Library of Congress Catalog Card Number: 86-12320

ISBN: 0–671–63923–4

First Pocket Books printing December 1987

10 9 8 7 6 5 4 3 2 1

POCKET and colophon are trademarks of
Simon & Schuster, Inc.

Printed in the U.S.A.

To the members of OSS and their Allied counterparts, who by their valiant covert and clandestine deeds, created an enviable legacy.
And to the U.S. Army Special Forces, who, founded on that glorious legacy, proudly guard it as their honored heritage.

# Contents

# Contents

# FROM OSS
# TO GREEN
# BERETS

# CHAPTER 1

# Initiation

"What a hellhole!" That was my first reaction to the sticky, humid heat that blanketed Camp Polk, Louisiana. I had recently been assigned as a tactical training officer to a railroad battalion stationed here.

This was quite a change from the usual intelligence duties I'd been assigned for most of my previous years of service. Desiring to obtain a troop assignment, I had requested to be released to my basic branch, which was infantry. However, since I was in my late thirties, the infantry relegated me to a training slot.

Dull work, I thought, considering that a war was on, although supposedly the railroad battalion was necessary. The men weren't interested in squad or platoon tactics. They were in uniform to run railroads. Only limited progress and results in military professionalism could be expected.

My spirits were low with such unrewarding duty, not to mention the devilish climate coupled with the oversized mosquitoes and the snakes that seemed to adore holing up in our sleeping bags.

That spring morning in 1943, as I passed the adjutant's tent, a notice on the bulletin board caught my eye. It announced that volunteers with foreign language capabilities would be interviewed for special assignments.

My pulse quickened; a ray of hope appeared. This could

be a way out. Did I have the qualifications required? Luckily I did. I had a background in French and German. My grandfather used to converse with me in German and my mother would do the same in French. They had emigrated from Russia. The family had been quite well-to-do and were well educated. My mother had received a secondary education in France. In addition, in my younger days, I had been the chief lifeguard and swimming instructor at a private beach in Biarritz, France, where I had to use French, German, and Spanish on a daily basis. So I asked the adjutant what the special assignments were all about. He didn't know, but he set me up for an interview.

Awaiting the day of the interview, I was on tenterhooks. My curiosity was aroused. The assignment must have something to do with intelligence or codes or liaison. Whatever, it could rescue me from my present situation.

I looked up several French Canadians who were in the outfit and started practicing French just to oil up my fluency, since I was getting a bit rusty. I hadn't had the occasion to speak anything but English in some time. I mentioned the request for language specialists but the battalion appeared indifferent. They were railroaders doing what was right down their alley. Obviously, they stuck with the old army adage: "Never volunteer for anything!" I had already decided to disregard this advice when I signed up to be interviewed.

On the appointed day, waiting my turn, I tried to appear at ease. But I was nervous. I did so want to be accepted. What if I failed? I'd be more in the dumps than ever. At last I was called. On entering the tent, I was greeted by a captain who, I felt, held my future in his hands. Would I make the grade? He recorded my personal history with great care and then tested my French. His fluency was more limited than mine, so he appeared quite impressed. I became enthused and kept spouting French.

Finally, he turned me off and posed the leading question. "Would you volunteer to operate behind the lines in uniform or civilian clothes?"

I was too anxious to consider the risks. I answered in the affirmative. That clinched it. He advised me that I would receive reassignment orders within the week.

I was in a state of euphoria, floating on a cloud, eagerly

awaiting my release from an unpleasant assignment. Certainly whatever was in store for me couldn't be any worse, with a good possibility of being a lot better. Little did I suspect the far-reaching consequences of that successful interview.

As the captain had said, my orders arrived in short order. They were quite brief. I was assigned to the Office of Strategic Services (OSS). I was to report to the Q Building in Washington, D.C. in civvies. At the time, I had no idea of the significance of OSS.

On arriving in Washington, D.C., garbed in a newly purchased pair of trousers and a polo shirt, I taxied to the Q Building, which was a fair distance from the railroad depot. As I entered the building, I noted a strong beery odor. Across the street was a local brewery spewing out that pervading malty aroma which enveloped the OSS headquarters and the rest of the neighborhood. However, it didn't appear to affect the doughty chairborne warriors.

The duty officer glanced at my orders and nonchalantly informed me that OSS was the Office of Strategic Services organized by Gen. William Donovan, a prominent New York attorney who was a highly decorated hero of World War I. His nickname was "Wild Bill." Whatever I would learn about OSS or see or hear concerning it was to be kept secret. The duty officer then directed me to report immediately to the Congressional Country Club. I started to ask questions on what sort of assignments were dished out and what the outfit did, but he was noncommittal.

"You'll get all that in your briefing and training," he told me. While I was gathering my gear and waiting for a taxi, I pondered over the type of missions OSS probably performed. Intelligence gathering, behind-the-lines raids, and long-range patrolling seemed possible, but the Army already had Rangers that handled such activities. Perhaps it was a super-Ranger setup, but that just didn't make sense.

Finally the cab arrived. I piled in with my gear and told the cabbie, "Congressional Country Club, please."

"What?" he said, turning his head and gazing at me. "Not another one of those guerrillas!"

What's all this crap about being so secret? Even the cabbies know all about it, I muttered to myself.

So that was the big secret—guerrilla warfare, resistance movements, and all that clandestine jazz! The cabbie had suddenly broadened my perspective. Where were the guerrillas operating? I had read about such operations in France, Yugoslavia, and Greece. That's where the language experience factor tied in!

At the club I was informed I would be briefed and assigned the next day. I noticed that the club had not been denuded of its civilian decor. The social rooms were still smartly decorated and the dining room, bar, and even the bedrooms were fully furnished. I was quartered in a room with twin beds and a private bath.

As I unpacked, I compared my present deluxe quarters with the bare tent, and its cot and footlocker, that I sweated in at Camp Polk. Since I had spare time, I started to do my daily exercise routine.

Suddenly the door opened and there stood a red-headed lieutenant, about my height and weight, which was five feet, eight and 155 pounds, who was evidently my roommate.

"Hey, what's going on?" he exclaimed.

"Just doing my daily workout. I'm Aaron Bank. Just got into town and got my 'top secret' briefing en route from the cab driver."

"I'm Bill Dreux. Got my original briefing the same way. When you're through, I'll introduce you to some of the guys," he responded as he sat down at the desk and watched my contortions.

After I'd showered and dressed, Bill showed me around the various wings of the clubhouse and the gorgeous golf course, which was now a training area. I met a number of officers. Among them were Bill Colby, who later became the director of the Central Intelligence Agency (CIA), and Lucien Conein, who also wound up in the CIA as a key agent in Vietnam. Al Cox and Serge Obalensky welcomed me, as did Cy Maniere, the only West-Pointer in the Operational Groups (OG's) at that time. Maniere was the CO of the group to which I would be assigned. Serge, of New York's Astor Hotel fame and a well-known socialite, had been an officer in the Russian (Tsar's) Army. Al Cox was the CO of the (OG's) section and continued on as chief when the OG's became a branch—the third leg of the OSS tripod of operational branches: Intelligence, Special Operations, and Operational Groups.

Our mess was in the resplendent dining room. Had it not been for the uniforms, I would have thought I was dining in the prerequisitioned Congressional Country Club.

The following day I was briefed. The briefing was directed almost solely to the OG section of OSS. Mention was made that OSS was operating in all areas of unconventional warfare (UW), which included covert and clandestine operations. The policy was that the less each operative knew about the organization, the tighter the security.

I was assigned to a French Operational Group (OG), the same to which Bill was also assigned. An OG consisted of thirty enlisted men and three officers split up into two fifteen-man sections. The mission was to infiltrate, usually by airdrop or by sea, enemy territory and join up with already-existing guerrilla bands and support them in conducting guerrilla warfare.

In our group was a mixture of linguists. Most, like me, had a telltale accent, although Bill, whose French parents had settled in New Orleans, was perfectly fluent with a true French accent. Also from Louisiana were some Cajuns who spoke their own dialect (patois) and French Canucks with their Quebec dialect. Their French was understandable except for the colloquialisms.

Most of the tactical training—conducted at the club and in the vicinity—was of the commando type. Emphasis was on raids, ambushes, cross-country movement, compass runs, sentry elimination, and the simulated destruction of various targets: bridges, culverts, railroads (trestles and tracks), canal locks, electric transformer stations, and high-tension-wire pylons. Night operations were stressed.

However, Bill and I were disappointed with this specialized infantry training. We felt cheated and not fully prepared to conduct all aspects of guerrilla warfare. We realized that there was much more to guerrilla warfare than commando operations, but there was no specialized training literature on the subject. Only experienced guerrilla fighters could fill this gap and, unfortunately, there weren't any available at the time.

There was one exception that cheered us somewhat, the

demolition training. This was conducted by an engineer officer who taught us how to destroy any type of guerrilla target. "Fire in the hole" (meaning the fuse is lit) became a standard part of our training vocabulary.

The most frustrating incidents would occur when, after painfully creeping and crawling through the underbrush to apply simulated plastic explosive charges to guarded road bridges and culverts, the nightly silence would be shattered by an all-too-familiar yell.

"There they are!" The harassment was imposed on us by the neighborhood kids who made a game out of spotting us. But it had been rumored that the guards passed out candy to sharpen their ears.

Before long, this harassment was avoided when we moved to a government reservation, a former Civilian Conservation Corps (CCC) camp near Quantico, Virginia. Here our exercises lasted longer and were more vigorous and we did perfect ourselves as commandos with a guerrilla flair. However, as I told Bill, "This still isn't the real McCoy."

Physically, the unit was in really good shape: no calisthenics, but good hard rope climbing, chinning, pushups with a knapsack on our back, and crossing streams on ropes slung horizontally between trees, topped off with five-plus miles of daily running. We had a good martial arts instructor and we specialized in knife fighting and throwing, a silent form of killing.

On my way from knife practice one day, I was subjected to the efficiency of that weapon. Swish! A knife flashed by my head and pinged into a tree with which I was lined up. I ducked and turned. There was one of our Canucks, who was really handy with the knife, grinning sheepishly at me.

"Sorry, sir. Didn't mean to come that close."

I walked over to the tree and retrieved the knife. "That's a nasty habit to get into. You'll have access to this toy only on the knife target area in the future," I said. With guys like that in the outfit, who needs the enemy? I mused as I walked on.

A few months later, back again in cushy quarters at the club, we had an officers' call. By that time, there were several additional operational groups quartered there.

Almost two dozen of us were assembled. A staff officer

from our Washington headquarters (HQ) notified us that an important, classified operation was being prepared in England to conduct unconventional warfare in France. It was expected to kick off much sooner than any OG-planned operation. As usual, volunteers were wanted. We had a break to discuss this after which, in spite of the old army adage, almost all volunteered.

"It pays to volunteer in this outfit," Bill observed laughingly. I agreed as I recalled Camp Polk.

# CHAPTER 2

# The Real McCoy

The move came fast. In October 1943, I, Bill, Conein, Cy Maniere, and some of the others shipped from New York on the old *Aquitania*, which was one of the fastest ocean liners at that time. Since she could outrun any U-boat, she crossed solo, instead of in slow convoy, without incident. However, we did have air cover for most of the crossing.

A week later, we reported in at OSS headquarters, London, located in Grosvenor Square, close to the U.S. Embassy in the fashionable Mayfair district. No one would have suspected that such a sedate, dignified-looking structure housed a cloak-and-dagger outfit: a headquarters where the most unconventional, daring schemes were developed into operational plans; the directing center of the U.S. participation in the "secret war."

Until we could be scheduled into the training program, we were quartered in a hotel in Piccadilly Circus. We got a chance to tour wartime, blacked-out London, already displaying cavities among the buildings on its streets from bombings and V-I rockets.

There were plenty of Yanks in the city, mostly Air Corps, frequenting the pubs and clubs at night. Around Piccadilly, where most of the nightly activity was centered, the numerous *femmes de joie* were shining blackout flashlights on our feet.

We asked some of the Air Corps fellows, who knew the ropes, about this practice.

"They're looking for jump boots, paratroopers. That extra jump pay makes them better-paying customers."

That explained all the "dearie" greetings we'd been receiving. Before we could get ourselves in a jam hanging around London, we were sent off to the first of the many schools we'd attend, and to a lengthy, close association with the British.

The school was in Scotland, some distance north of the Caledonian Canal. We were met at the railroad station in Arasaig by a major in kilts, who delivered us to a secret training center in a medium-size manor house, where we were quartered. It was around 4:30 P.M. when we arrived. We were ushered into the mess and served scones, omelets, jam, and tea. We were hungry and pitched in ravenously. I thought it was odd to have dinner served so early, but no matter; when hungry—eat!

We settled down; met our British instructors, who had seen action with Yugoslav, Greek, or French guerrillas; and were given copies of the training program. They were all Special Operations Executive (SOE) personnel. SOE, coordinating with OSS, was running these clandestine schools.

To our surprise, we were called to dinner around seven that evening. The British ran a good officers' mess, booze included. But in spite of the inviting dishes, the afternoon snack (high tea) had stunted our appetites and we couldn't do dinner justice.

The following day, after a hearty breakfast, our training started. At eleven we had a break with a sandwich and cocoa. Then we had lunch at noon; tea around 4:30 in the afternoon, when training ended; and, of course, dinner in the evening. We had reached the limit. We couldn't handle it. We were bursting at the seams trying to keep up. How these Britishers could eat so damn much and still stay lean was beyond us. We'd have to work out all day long to do it. So we stuck to our habitual three meals a day from then on.

At the British school, we were truly starting to delve into certain aspects of UW. We would cover guerrilla formations and tactics, enemy weapons, and guerrilla type of demolitions. Although our demolition training stateside had been good, this course was presented in greater detail with a larger variety of explosive gadgets and fuses.

"Now we are getting the real McCoy," I exulted to the others. They all agreed.

After a few weeks, the Scottish major took some of us on a map-reading and compass run. He gave us a brief history of Scotland during lunch break. When he finished, he was asked about kilts.

"Well, you've evidently noticed that you've been wading through a lot of streams, getting your trousers pretty soaked, and they're still dripping. I admit, my shoes are wet, but check my bare legs. They're dry. That's the reason for our kilt custom."

He never did tell us if he wore anything under the kilts. That's still an unsolved mystery to me.

On another occasion, on a hunt with the major, one of us shot a deer. The major had a canvas folding bucket along, which I had noticed but hadn't been able to explain. He slit the throat of the animal and let the blood flow into the bucket. When it was full, he stood up with the bucket in his hands and approached the chap who had shot the deer.

"Now I'm going to pay you the honors due on shooting your first deer." With that, he poured the blood on the hapless victim. However, this was no whim on the part of the major. It was an old Scottish rite and really considered an honor.

This same bloke, as we called him, taught an interesting ammunition course. He trained us so that even in the dark, just feeling a cartridge, we could tell the caliber and for which weapon it was designed. We thought it was nice to know, but never would be of any practical use. Later, when operational, I found out otherwise.

The next school that we shifted to in the Midlands offered training in Intelligence; agent activities; forming resistance and guerrilla movements; and operating various types of networks—sabotage, subversion, security, escape and evasion, and counterespionage. Included also were other related subjects of which we had never been aware, some of which currently are classed as terrorism.

Another school specialized in raids and advanced sabotage with stress on railroads. Here we had the opportunity to apply simulated charges on locomotives and coal tenders and actually blow up sections of railroad tracks on an unused spur. We were introduced to the use of simulated coal made of plastic explosive. When these chunks, surreptitiously mixed with the coal in the locomotive tender, were shoveled into the boiler, they would explode and rupture it. We also had goods (freight) cars on which to practice. Pouring sand into the hot boxes (axle-grease boxes) would freeze the wheels. We learned how to disconnect the cars and even how to drive a locomotive. One of our crew, in forward instead of reverse gear, inadvertently drove through the brick wall of the round-house.

The turntable of a roundhouse was a profitable sabotage target. If the support column was blown, the turntable couldn't turn and match up its tracks with those running from the roundhouse. Consequently, all garaged locomotives couldn't be driven out to be utilized without extensive repairs to the turntable.

All this practice was whetting our appetite for the real thing. We were starting to get eager for action, but the rehearsals continued.

In practicing raids we had to clear buildings up to three stories high of aggressor details. The British had it down to a science. The secret was to control the halls and stairways while the assault teams cleared the rooms. While in school near London, we attended the raid and street-fighting center on the outskirts of the capital. We raided five- and six-story buildings which represented large military headquarters. We cleared mock towns. We appreciated learning these raiding techniques, but thought we'd never be engaged in street fighting. Again, I learned otherwise.

The next-to-the-last school we attended specialized in communications. We were instructed in encoding and decoding cipher codes and in operating long-range radios using Morse code. This was the toughest of all. We'd practice all day long, day after day, until we were proficient enough to act as basic operators if our team operator was eliminated. The instruction was handled by the FANYS or the Female Auxiliary Nursing Yeomanry. This was an excellent service whose members also performed clerical duties and packed parachutes. The more mechanically inclined even worked in motor pools.

Our final stint was at Ringway, the British jump school. Their system of training was low key. Right off, you were told that jumping was only a mode of transportation and not a bold heroic act.

To show how simple it really was, our instructor, on the day we were to start taking our five qualifying jumps, told us, "First, you'll see a couple of French female agents jump and then a sixty-five-year-old Frenchman, also in agent training."

We witnessed these jumps and, after the participants had landed and brought their chutes to the packing shed, we talked to them while they were drinking their cocoa—a reward for those who walked away from the jump. We also noted that the Frenchman was wearing only sneakers, making us feel sheepish when we looked at our spit-and-polish jump boots.

"You'll jump out of the gondola of a balloon for your first jump, three to a trip," announced the instructor.

It was only then that we noticed a balloon tied to a cable which was coiled around a winch.

Bill, I, and another of our group got into the gondola and sat around the jump hole. We were trained to jump not out of the door but out of a hole in the fuselage of a plane. This was the type of jumping used for agents and clandestine operatives. The hole was wide enough for only one man at a time to drop through the bottom of the funnel, although three could sit around the upper part. It was imperative to remember your jump sequence number, otherwise trouble! The balloon was allowed to rise.

When my number was called, I pushed off and exited properly at the position of attention. But after counting for three seconds, I didn't feel any shock of the chute opening. I kept falling for about 200 feet before I noticed the chute billowing out. Guiding myself with the risers, I aimed for the packing shed and cocoa stand. I made an easy landing, but I was mentally shocked.

"What the hell held up my chute from opening sooner?" I demanded of the instructor.

He laughed. "You're all in the same boat, no prop blast of a plane to open the canopy in a hurry." He explained that

22

jumping out of a still balloon held in place at 800 feet altitude by a cable requires a drop of around 200 feet to meet enough air resistance to expand and float the canopy.

However, I still felt shaky about it because the British system did not include a reserve chute. Recovering, I facetiously asked him, "What the devil do we do if the chute doesn't open?"

He responded in the same vein. "After you land, roll up your chute and take it back to the FANY who packed it and see if she'll give you a date!" It was a matter-of-fact course.

# CHAPTER 3

# The Jedburghs

After all the individual training was completed, we departed for Peterborough, about ninety miles north of London. Our secret area, a few miles outside the city, was the requisitioned estate of a coal baron. It extended for acres. Its manor house, Milton Hall, had been constructed in the seventeenth century. Actually a small castle, it had about fifty rooms and its gray stone walls were at least a couple of feet thick.

On this estate we would conduct team training and stage for our operation. First we would be briefed, since we still had no idea of what the operation was called or what it entailed. We would also meet a lot of unknowns, since the British, French, Belgian, and Dutch personnel who had also volunteered had been undergoing the same training we had just completed but at different time periods.

It all reminded me of a bunch of schoolboys returning to boarding school for the coming semester. We spent the first few days just meeting one another. French was heard everywhere. We got acquainted with our headquarters and the ample grounds and were assigned our rooms, six officers to a room. In ours, it just happened that we were a mixture of British and Americans and we had a young but sharp batman who would take care of all our wants: housekeeping, laundry, ironing, shining boots, cleaning our field gear, and so forth. He was paid an extra stipend of a shilling a week by each of us. For that emolument he also awakened us with a mug of tea and a "Good morning, sir." This function he coordinated with the crack-of-dawn wailing of bagpipes, piped by a Scotch Highlander stomping through the corridors.

The atmosphere was Elizabethan with paneled walls and oak-beamed ceilings. In the corridors, Cromwellian armor, swords, and shields competed for space and the clank of armor from bygone days was echoed by the pounding of our boots. It was truly a warrior's domain.

Finally, we were assembled in the large, baronial hall for the briefing. We were introduced to the station commander, Colonel Spooner, an Indian Army type, ramrod straight and a true disciplinarian. Then the commander of the Americans, Lt. Col. Dick Musgrove, a pleasant, mild-mannered Virginian, was presented. He handled all the administration pertaining to the American Jeds.

The briefing was conducted by a British lieutenant colonel who was chief of training and was usually teamed with Musgrove to check our training.

We were informed that the operation was named the "Jedburgh Mission."* It would be composed of numerous three-man teams which would be infiltrated by air (parachute) primarily into occupied France, and also Belgium and Holland, prior to D day to organize the guerrilla potential and conduct unconventional warfare with emphasis on guerrilla warfare. This called for large-scale guerrilla activity with all-out attacks on the Germans starting on D day to disrupt communications; ambush convoys; destroy the rail track system, road bridges, trestles, and culverts; and delay reinforcements headed for the invasion area.

For the French operation each team, due to the insistence of General de Gaulle, would have a French officer.

To service the entire operation—basically a tripartite effort of the SOE, OSS, and Bureau Central de Renseignements et Action (BCRA)—around 350 officers and enlisted men of the combined services were assembled. The OSS contingent con-

---

* The name "Jedburgh" was derived from the twelfth century border wars between the Scots and the British invaders in the Jedburgh area of Scotland where a local Scottish group conducted guerrilla warfare.

sisted of 53 officers and 40 enlisted men. The enlisted men of all the agencies represented were radio operators.

Each team had two officers and one enlisted radio operator. The leader would be the ranking officer.

Initially, until temporary teams could be formed, individual training would continue. This was a rehash of everything we'd been through.

Most of the training was conducted within the estate. Demolition charges were shaking the grounds and small-arms firing resounded from the area where fashionable ladies had played croquet. This is where Major Fairbairn, a British expert in the martial arts and the developer, with his partner Captain Sykes, of the famous Fairbairn–Sykes fighting knife, held sway with his instruction in instinctive firing. This was a method by which you aimed a handgun with your body rather than with your eyes on the sights—a specialty for night combat. Major Fairbairn was also highly visible in the sunken gardens where we practiced silent killing with the use of the knife or the garrote. Knife fighting was included. However, rather than the smell of blood, we'd inhale the fragrance of roses and the boxwood hedges. All day long the da-de-da of Morse code could be heard floating out of the library windows where we'd take turns tapping the sending keys.

No time was lost; everything we should know was packed in. As a bonus, we had a lovely—in my opinion, beautiful—FANY teaching encoding and decoding. Some of the younger bucks always raced in at the start of the period to sit up front and be really close to her. With practically the whole gang to choose from, she took a shine to one of the French officers who came from an affluent family in Guatemala. Guy had been an amateur boxer and looked it. This eventually led to fisticuffs between Guy and one of the Americans who hadn't clicked with our charming instructor. Before we could break it up, Guy sparkled. He sure knew how to use his dukes!

We were parachuting regularly, mostly night jumps and always out of the Joe-hole. I became quite accustomed to it, but we still carried no reserve chute.

Major Fairbairn pulled a fast one on us. He waited for a really dark, moonless night and had us called out for sentry elimination training. We had been taught how to approach a sentry from the rear, snap an arm around his neck in a choke hold, and thrust a stiletto of Fairbairn design between his upper ribs while bending him backward. When it came my turn, I approached the dummy, grasped it, and bent it back as I plunged my knife into, of all things, a knapsack instead of the ribs. Had this been for keeps, the sentry would not have been eliminated. All our previous practice had been on dummies without a knapsack. Fairbairn drove his point home. We never forgot. You had to determine before the attack whether a knapsack was being worn. A two-man elimination team was the safest and quietest, since one man effected the assault while the other grasped the sentry's rifle before it dropped, clattering, to the ground.

There were a number of other no-nos drilled into us. In a raid, never attempt to enter a room without a full magazine in your pistol or submachine gun and don't stand in the doorway. Don't fool around with the local women, particularly if they are in the Resistance or a guerrilla organization. Don't split an ambush unit onto either side of a road. They'll wind up shooting into one another. Don't concentrate forces; keep them well dispersed. Don't slug it out with the enemy; hit and run. There were others, but these stand out.

When we weren't on a night exercise, we dined in the paneled dining hall. The food was served on large platters and in deep bowls placed on the refectory tables by mess attendants. The British ran the mess and furnished the household troops. Beer and liquor were available as in any officers' club. The food was passed around the table and there was always a considerable quantity. The meats were plainly prepared. But in typical English style, the vegetables or greens were pressed solid like a cake. Of course, with the blockade on, we had only powdered eggs, canned milk, tea (good-bye coffee!), mostly canned fruit and vegetables, and a little fresh, but mostly canned, meat.

However, no matter what the makings for a meal consisted of, the French knew how to dress it up. It wasn't long before they invaded the kitchen and, instead of teaching the cockney cooks how to poison the enemy, they taught them a smattering of gourmet cooking. Prodded by this coaching, the repasts became tastier, but, with the spiced sauces camouflaging the food, you didn't always know what you were eating.

Associated with this gastronomical effort, another French

27

custom was introduced. Each evening, one of the junior French officers would read the menu in French, announcing the most fabulous and delectable dishes. However, he'd have to hypnotize you to make those actually served taste like the ones called for on the menu.

Right after being awakened every morning, we'd line up for our daily run. We'd polish off four to five miles, but at a hell of a pace. The British physical training sergeants, headed by Master Sergeant Fernandez, kept us hopping. If you loitered, one of them would be right with you, urging you on in no uncertain terms. "On with you, sir." But if it were Fernandez, you'd have his knees, pumping like pistons, on your rump. And you really ticked him off if you called him sergeant instead of master sergeant.

Following the run, we'd be paired in groups of six. Each group would exercise in unison with a tree trunk, pressing it overhead and curling it—wholesale weight lifting. The training sergeants kept us in shape by being polite but firm.

With all that exercise, plus a lot of cross-country hiking, we built up a terrific appetite. However, I noticed that one of the Britishers with whom we were quite close was suddenly just nibbling at his food during mealtime. Nevertheless, he surreptitiously filched nonperishable items from the table and placed them in his pockets.

I was puzzled and casually asked him, "Reggie, how come?"

He nonchalantly responded that he enjoyed eating later in his room and so it rested.

A few days later, while on an exercise, several of us stumbled upon a small civilian type of tent pitched in a clearing. We approached it cautiously, wondering why it was in the secret training area. Upon flipping the tent flap, we gazed upon a lovely feminine creature reclining on a spread-out bedding roll. She immediately volunteered that she was Reggie's lady friend and was visiting for a few days. We backed away, wished her pleasant camping, and decided that Reggie was quite an operator! Of course, we had discovered Reggie's invisible dinner guest!

But we didn't know how good an operator he was! Several weeks later, a few of us were invited to a gathering at the home of a parson in Peterborough. It was located on the par-ish grounds. We had permission from stiff-backed Colonel Spooner to attend.

When we arrived the clergyman greeted us warmly and while he was introducing us to his guests we noted, much to our surprise, none other than Reggie and his lady friend coming down from upstairs. Our host was overjoyed when he saw them.

"I want you to meet Captain and Mrs. Carlton. They're my weekend guests." We greeted them cordially and determined that sly Reggie was, without a doubt, the best operator in the outfit.

Repeating our training in the entire spectrum of subjects related to unconventional warfare had honed us to an almost combat state of perfection. The time was ripe for extensive maneuvers to truly test our ability. That meant the formation of the permanent, three-man teams.

At first it was decided to allow the training staff to pair up the teams. But that idea was quickly dropped when we convinced Colonel Musgrove and his British counterpart that, since we now knew one another quite well, we'd be better qualified to set up these partnerships by mutual consent. In this way we'd obtain maximum compatibility.

However, there was a fly in the ointment. There had to be a French officer on each team for the French operation, but there weren't sufficient officers available to take care of the more numerous British and Americans. The process, instead of being classed as a dignified courtship and marriage, turned into a frenzied scramble.

It became a competitive struggle. We, as well as the British, battled it out man to man, trying either to tie up with a Frenchman who was our senior or to entice a junior-ranking officer to join up with us.

But it was the French who made the determination. They were the ones being courted, regardless of rank. They could pick and choose and had fun doing it. They played hard to get.

Among us, my buddy Bill had the easiest time of it since he spoke fluent, colloquial French. That was an all-important ingredient in establishing compatibility and understanding. Several of the British were also in the same category, not language-wise but in combat experience with well-earned decorations.

There was a quiet little French lieutenant with whom I had struck up an acquaintance. I knew him only as Henri. (Forty years later, in June 1984, at the Jedburgh reunion in Paris, I finally discovered, by his disclosure, that Denis was his family name.)

Although only a lieutenant myself, I approached him with a proposal to join up with me. But Henri appeared undecided and backed off. His attitude toward me cooled. I felt just as rebuffed as any suitor whose girl had turned him down.

I held off a few days. During this period, I noticed him being approached by others. Wanting to be a team leader, I again pursued him. The colonel had approved two consecutive weekends in London to assist us in cementing teams.

With this opportunity, I jumped on the bandwagon and invited Henri to spend the weekends with me—I should say on me—in London. He accepted and then he put me through the wringer. That meant the best hotels, the most expensive French restaurants, and ladies of the evening. The price was high!

I put up with all this, hoping he would finally agree to our partnership, or I should say marriage. That devil kept me on tenterhooks until our return from the final weekend, when he agreed. Later, he told me that he was just testing me and would have joined up with me regardless. He had a point. I did appreciate him more after expending all that effort; it did increase my respect for him.

He proved to be a capable, loyal teammate. Initially we had an American sergeant named Bill Thompson as our radio operator, but later he was switched for a French operator. As I recall, it was because of the language barrier between Bill and Henri. Being a crack radio operator, Bill was snatched up by another team and went on to merit the croix de guerre. Our new operator's name was Jean. None of the French ever used their family name for security reasons, since their families were in France.

Once the teams were formed, we conducted preliminary exercises to shake us down, devise team operating procedures, determine areas of responsibility, and really get to know one another in the field. We also needed to smooth out any language problems in the handling of codes in radio communications with the base station.

In sorting out the areas of responsibility for our team, I charged Henri with:

A. Handling all political problems endemic to the French Resistance and the Maquis (active guerrilla groups), mainly between de Gaulle's Forces Françaises de l'Intérieur (FFI) and the Francs-Tireurs Partisans (FTP)—Communists.
B. Supervising the formation of clandestine networks and their operation.
C. Assisting me in training the networks.
D. Maintaining liaison with networks in adjacent areas and cooperating with friendly municipal and other officials.

As team leader, apart from overall responsibility, I would be mainly concerned with the formation of the guerrilla units and their training, arming, and operation; overall planning; sifting tactical from strategic intelligence; and making contact with regional resistance leaders. I would also handle the reception of airdrops and their distribution: Henri would be charged with the setup of the reception committee, security, and transportation. The radio operator would be solely occupied with codes and radio communications, maintenance of his equipment, and transportation of it.

Since Henri spoke and understood just a minimum of English, we communicated almost totally in French. This improved my speaking ability and also broadened my military vocabulary.

Team maneuvers were now conducted at intervals. A certain number of teams were on night problems on alternate schedules. That put us in the field on an average of three nights a week during this final training phase. However, some of the teams became divorced, finding that they weren't really compatible. Thus new ones were formed. This all served to solidify us into truly permanent partnerships.

There was always a target to hit with simulated plastic charges which, when we were successful, were taped on. At times, the guard element was too alert and resourceful and we'd risk capture.

The enemy was represented by the household troops and guard elements from Milton Hall, backed by the Home Guard and local police.

After hitting a sabotage target, the chase would be on: a bit of "Hare and Hounds." The enemy knew and checked all the likely hiding places in the neighborhood: the woods, deserted barns, road culverts, haystacks—anywhere. It was a constant effort to avoid being picked up. On the move all the time, we were fortunate we didn't have to take our heavy suitcase radios with us on these exercises.

The exercise area included a number of large estates, many with ancient manor houses. While on the run one night, I observed an estate I thought would be the last place the enemy would look for us. Henri agreed and our radio operator added his approval, "Epatant!" We headed for the closest manor house on the estate, approaching it carefully and wondering if the local police had alerted the residents to inform them if any soldiers were roaming around.

We decided to gamble that they hadn't and pulled the bell clapper. It was only around 9 P.M. and people would still be up. The butler answered the door and looked wide-eyed at one man in a U.S. jump uniform and two attired in French military garb, all three dusty and dirty.

"Come in, gentlemen. I will notify the family."

The head of the household greeted us warmly after we explained that we belonged to a special Allied unit that was conducting exercises.

"The butler will show you to your rooms. Be our guests overnight."

We were escorted to two rooms—our radio operator to a single one and Henri and I to a large, lavishly decorated one. We dunked ourselves in a hot tub, told the butler to get us on our way before daylight, and hit the sack, enjoying the cool sheets and soft mattresses.

After a hearty breakfast, we thanked our butler friend and departed with his "Good luck, chaps! Come again."

Not only had he awakened us with the usual cup of tea, but had also laundered our uniforms, polished our boots, and given us a bag of sandwiches to tide us over.

However, I didn't think that it was a good idea to present such a neat, polished appearance. The umpires of the exercise would become suspicious. Therefore we deliberately dirtied our uniforms and boots, but only after we were out of sight. In no way did we want to dull the ardor of that patriotic butler.

During the maneuver period, on more than one occasion we resorted to this procedure. But we dropped it when the training staff started wondering how we had been able to avoid capture for so long.

There was one weak link in all this training. We were doing the work that would be done by the guerrillas and sabotage agents we'd train. Thus we weren't getting the practice we needed in leading and coordinating guerrilla troops. This could have been accomplished by scattering the available troops at Milton Hall in small groups within the exercise area to represent the guerrilla potential. We could have infiltrated by air or on foot to organize and train them and then have them conduct the action under our supervision.

On our free nights, we would often gather in the drawing room, which served more or less as our officers' club. Some of the Britishers were accomplished pianists and we'd have a singing session.

Among the three nationalities, it was the British who had the best repertoire of songs. They had the old ballads, the popular rags, and their glorious regimentals. But the standouts were the bawdy, rollicking ones. They had numerous verses, each rendered by a different individual, at the end of which everyone would join in the chorus. There was one based on *The Arabian Nights*. That was a corker! But the spiciest was *The Ball of Kerrymuir,* with more than a hundred verses and a ripsnorting chorus that was unforgettable and in which everyone delighted in joining. In fact, it's only the tail end of the chorus that I now remember but must refrain from repeating. When the call "Come on, Yanks!" came, we'd sheepishly respond with such weak fare (in comparison to theirs) as *My Old Kentucky Home, The Caissons Go Rolling Along,* or *Alouette.*

Finally, the staff considered us honed to action capability and the training slacked off. Rumors that a certain number of teams would be shipped to North Africa started circulating.

Since Henri had seen service in Africa, in the Senegal, and, at the outbreak of war, in Algiers, we realized that most likely we would be among them. And since this was the end of the training phase, we decided to go through a compressed review of the major guerrilla tactics.

This we did with one of the bilingual instructors who also invited Bill and his French partner Major Jean-Paul and a few other teams.

We selected the most important operations that we could anticipate, such as ambushes; raids; house clearing; and destruction of targets to include bridges, electric transformers, power plant turbines, railroad turntables, high-tension transmission pylons, and the railroad track system.

Riding bicycles, we'd take a tactical ride, stop at pertinent locations, and discuss the methods and tactics we'd employ, such as choosing for an ambush part of a road that was at a long curve, with an embankment on one side and a declining slope on the other. Approach and withdrawal would be reconnoitered in advance, with each route different and out of sight of towns and away from farmhouses. A reassembly area would be selected along the withdrawal route. We would plan how to stop the lead vehicle of a convoy—with the Pioneer Infantry Anti-Tank (PIAT) or a land mine (plastic charge) in the road or a gammon grenade.

Discussion on raids and target destruction always stressed the breakdown of the unit involved. There would be a sentry-eliminating element, followed by the attack or demolition team(s) with the security element placed in position to hold up the approach of the guard reserves. And a recce (abbreviation for reconnaissance) of the target and sentry system was a must, even if only at a distance with field glasses. Surprise was always the most required ingredient.

"Where would you apply charges to blow that bridge?" The instructor was pointing at a railroad trestle.

We indicated the center vertical support and estimated the thickness of the piling, the amount of the plastic charge, and the function of the security element in eliminating the guards in case of discovery.

"Give me the setup to raid this building if used as a Gestapo headquarters." It was a three-story town hall.

One of the group answered. "Sentry-elimination team;

room-clearing team for each floor; stair-landing detail per floor with a zone of fire down the hallway; lanes of fire set up outside, covering sides and exits of the building and the main security element sealing off the approach route of reserves.''

Others added signals used when killer teams exited from each room into the hallway or building, since anyone exiting a room or the building would be shot if the correct signal hadn't been given.

''What location is best to blast railroad tracks?'' We were grouped along the railroad right-of-way.

''On a curve,'' someone answered.

''About how much and how?''

''About six to eight feet of track on either side, by setting a detonator on each track so that the train will set off the charges,'' someone else responded.

Thus these tactical rides served to cover most of the typical situations we wished to review concerning guerrilla tactics. They ensured that we had an in-depth knowledge of all the aspects.

The instructor appeared pleased. ''Gentlemen, you're ready, but remember that your intended role is to train guerrillas to carry out these functions, not to do them yourselves.''

But a flaw appeared when I inquired what action should be taken when our force was in an ambush position, awaiting a reported enemy convoy, and peasants stumbled into it.

The instructor was stymied. ''Use your own judgment,'' was his only reply.

Later, when such a situation arose, I found a workable solution, something that should have been experienced in training.

We had a series of talks by individuals, both French and British, just recently returned from France. All of them dealt with La Résistance: how to organize; keeping networks separated, with each network cell compartmented; the use of couriers, each one responsible for three to five cells of two to three agents each and for their recruitment, training, and supplies; and how to train the couriers in the maintenance of network security and in the area of safe houses, letter drops, and clandestine meetings.

Since I had listed the formation and operation of networks as one of his responsibilities, Henri asked a considerable number of questions during the question-and-answer periods. I was pleased at his serious interest, because I intended to make maximum use of such nets. I recognized them as the ears and eyes of the active guerrilla groups (the Maquis) and realized that they could operate in urban areas where guerrilla activities would usually not be feasible.

These sessions stressed the use of passive as well as active sabotage. The reason was that the passive type could not always be pinpointed as actual sabotage and that in some cases it was more feasible. For example, to induce factory workers to malinger they'd be taught the symptoms of various ailments. Faking these would get them intermittently excused from working or would permit them to work at a much reduced pace, turning out machine parts that were flawed or had the wrong measurements. Sand or other abrasives would be put in lubricating oil and in the oil reservoirs of turbines, generators, and other machinery. Machine lathes would be filed in spots so that they'd tear after short usage. Railroad workers poured sand in the freight car axle-lubricating boxes; fouled up the signal system; and switched cars onto the wrong spurs and tracks, thus misdirecting shipments. Negligent maintenance took its toll on locomotives. Passive sabotage and functioning in the escape and evasion networks to rescue downed Allied pilots gave thousands of patriotic Frenchmen the chance to do their share toward the liberation of France, with fewer risks than those faced by the active saboteurs and guerrillas.

Radio and code training continued, but basically we had reached the staging phase. We were all getting anxious; it was time for action. When would the operation start?

As I recollect, it was around the middle of April 1944 when the order was posted. We were among the dozen or so teams being transferred to Algiers. It was really no surprise. With Henri's background, we had figured that, if the rumor proved true, we'd be on our way. That night we had a bash. We bade farewell to the gang. We had so many close friends among all the nationalities—friendships that had been cemented during months of training, brawling, and close association. Being in a generous mood, I grossly overpaid my batman for his last week's service, which most likely spoiled him, forcing my former roommates to up the ante.

At Liverpool, we boarded ship. "Shades of the Congressional Country Club!" I exclaimed as we passed through the social rooms on the upper deck.

The *Capetown Castle,* which was British, formerly had been a passenger liner on the South African run. It had not been transformed into a troop ship. Like the club, it had all its peacetime decor: paneled lounges, dining room, bar, card rooms, library. Even the expensive oil paintings were still in evidence as well as luxuriant furnishings and soft carpets. The cabins were generally deluxe.

Among the American Jeds, we recalled the Congressional Country Club days and agreed that OSS intermittently offered plush fare. "Join OSS and go first class!"

By that time, some of the critics of OSS were dubbing it *"Oh So Social."* Since its administrative and staff echelons were loaded with socialites, it was becoming a status symbol.

We were bunked four officers to a cabin and couldn't have asked for more as far as comfortable quarters were concerned.

Although we were separate, operational teams, we shipped as a unit with the senior Jed in command, who was Maj. Hod Fuller, a Marine turned Jed. He suggested that we take a daily workout on deck, but at no specified time. Henri didn't think much of calisthenics, but he did stomp around the deck. However, the American Jeds and some of the British and French complied regularly by indulging in either shadowboxing, calisthenics, or jogging or in a combination thereof, as I did.

We continued our radio-sending and -receiving training on telegraph keys that we had brought along. Some of the radio operators would tap out messages in Morse code, which we'd translate into words and take turns sending. Of course, the sound of the da-de-da signals were heard by passersby in the passageways. It wasn't long before a couple of British MP's and a ship's officer dashed into our cabin to see what was up. It had been reported that a secret radio was in operation in our cabin. The result was that radio training was discontinued.

Unfortunately, we American Jeds had packed only combat gear in our rucksacks and duffel bags. That meant we had only the regulation jump uniforms. The first night at sea we noted that the Americans were the only officers in the resplendent dining room not attired in service uniforms.

The senior British officer, a colonel, sent a message for the major to report to him. The colonel directed that we dress in service or dress uniform for dinner in the future. The major offered our apologies and explained that we had only jump uniforms. This sufficed, but it was evident that the colonel was displeased. Hod told us that the colonel was a "chairborne" staff officer, an "old fuddy-duddy," and to forget it.

When we were within several days of reaching port and enjoying cruising through the mild, lovely, blue Mediterranean, Hod was again called in by the colonel.

"Sports Day tomorrow. How about entering your Americans in a boxing tournament? They seem to be in excellent physical condition. I've noticed them taking daily, vigorous workouts."

Not suspecting any ulterior motive in the proposition and thinking that it would improve relations with "old fuddy-duddy," Hod agreed.

The next day we were escorted to the butcher shop to be weighed in. While this was going on, I noticed some hard, tough-looking characters lolling in the passageway, stripped to the waist and in shorts. When I inquired who those chaps were, I was told they were the blokes we were going to box. We started to feel a bit ill at ease since they looked too professional. After we were weighed in, we asked to meet them. They were called over and the referee, a sergeant in the Royal Marines, presented them. We shook hands and wished each other the best. We didn't recognize any of them since they were all crew members. Among them were fleet championship runners-up in the welterweight and middleweight class, the light-heavyweight champ of the Royal Marine Mediterranean Contingent, and standouts in other classes. By now, we were more than a bit ill at ease. We knew we were in for it!

I looked up our still-unsuspecting Hod and gave him the facts. "We've been had! That so-called old fuddy-duddy outfoxed you. He's going to square things up his own way!"

Hod looked blank. "Sort of a sticky wicket. I thought the tournament would be between officers."

"This is more than sticky. Some of us are going to get pasted!" When I said that, I was thinking of myself, approaching forty. Although still adept at the dirty tricks rough-and-tumble style, that ability long since had been restricted by the Marquis of Queensberry.

What I had predicted was exactly what happened. We took a good pasting except for our French pal, Guy, Hod's teammate, who knew how to use his dukes and had volunteered to participate with us, and (Mac) Austin, who gave as much as he received. At dinner the colonel offered a toast to the spunky Americans, but that didn't improve our swollen knuckles and spot-taped faces.

As we entered Oran Harbor, something far more serious, as far as national relations were concerned, occurred. There were a number of buoys shaped like headstones. Actually, it was the graveyard of the French fleet that had been sunk by the British when the Vichy government refused to ally it with them. The French and British Jeds were silent, but there was a chilly atmosphere that didn't thaw for some time.

When we arrived at Algiers, the British and American SOE and OSS station chiefs greeted us with stares and were overheard declaring that brawling and drinking among the Americans had to stop: a souvenir of Sports Day!

We were trucked to our base which was again on a private estate. It was staffed by Algerian soldiers who evidently had no regard for normal military sanitation. Scraps of toilet paper were dotting the landscape, indicating that they had relieved themselves alfresco rather than at a common latrine.

"God damn it!" I blurted out to Hod Fuller. "Those bastards are going to run our mess and we'll wind up with the pip [diarrhea]."

He agreed emphatically. He complained to OSS headquarters and, although the grounds were policed, the mess remained just that—messy. The kitchen had primitive refrigeration, and perishable food was left lying around among hordes of flies. We never felt comfortable at meals and grumbled about the situation, but we had to put up with it.

"Nothing like the old Congressional Country Club or even Milton Hall. This is the pits!" was the consensus.

To keep us occupied, we conducted various exercises and long-range compass and map-orientation runs. We'd be dropped off at night in the Atlas Mountains with instructions to be at base within two to four days, depending on the distance. This was in isolated, rugged country with few trails and Arab villages.

Henri was a whiz at map reading. He could easily orient a corresponding terrain feature to one on the map, then study *la carte* for a few minutes and never glance at it again, regardless of the constant detours to avoid gullies and canyons.

"How the hell do you do it, Henri?"

"Oh, I just have a good bump of direction," he'd say with a grin as I'd check the map at each detour.

Although Henri was tops with a map, he was low on water discipline.

"Henri, quit carrying wine in your canteen instead of water," I'd caution.

But he'd indulge himself anyway. Algeria was a land of wine, albeit not the best vintages. And he knew my extremely conservative use of water, which meant he could depend on bumming some from me when the wine gave out. He always claimed, "Water's all right for washing, not drinking!"

Then a big maneuver came off involving all French units. We were deployed as guerrillas, but the teams were based at a common bivouac area and accompanied by a flock of sheep which was our meat supply for the duration of the exercise.

There were specific targets to hit, guarded by Spahis, the native cavalry. We were spotted at one of those targets, a large electric transformer station, and were pursued by Spahis on their snorting Arab steeds. We were captured after being clouted with the broadsides of their sabers.

"Ils ne jouent pas du tout," I glumly observed.

"Ils sont des braves types." Henri appeared to be proud to have been manhandled by them. He looked upon them in the sàme light as the native troops with whom he had served in the Senegal. *"Mes enfants,"* as he would refer to them nostalgically.

40

Between exercises, except for Morse-code training, we did a bit of swimming at the Algerian beaches and roamed around the city. Henri had friends residing there and we were always welcome.

One day, while being trucked back to the base, we noticed a guy, in what looked like a sports shirt and shorts, running on the sidewalk in the outskirts of the city in the direction of our base. As we got closer, we saw people gazing at him quizzically because, of all things, he was in his underwear and barefoot. When we caught up with him, we recognized him as one of our Jeds.

"What the hell's cooking?" we called to him.

"My babe's husband came home unexpectedly and I had to scram sans uniform and boots. How about a lift?"

We just laughed and waved, letting him finish his amorous adventure as he had started it—on his own.

Nobody knew when the Mediterranean invasion of France would occur. The Normandy invasion had already taken place, on 6 June, and only a few weeks had passed. We were starting to have misgivings that we might miss the boat. Only two of the teams had been infiltrated—Captain Austin's and Major MacPherson's (a Britisher)—and we were becoming doubtful whether we would get in at all. Would the mission be scratched?

A dose of fever, lasting three or four days, made its appearance in camp. The French weren't affected, but the British and the Americans were. One by one, we were hit and taken to the military hospital in Algiers.

On my second day there, while dozing in bed, in rushed Henri. "Nous sommes en alerte pour cette nuit!"

The shock of that explosive statement rejuvenated me. I propelled myself out of bed and sped to the clothes locker only to find my uniform and boots missing.

Time was of the essence. We had lots to do in order to be operationally ready for takeoff.

"Allons-y! I'll just go in pajamas."

We exited from my room and walked through the wards until we reached the entrance foyer. A couple of British MP's were on duty outside the entrance.

"Où est la voiture?" I asked Henri.

He told me where his jeep was parked. "Jean est au volant et il n'a pas coupé le moteur."

It would be a gamble if we could reach the jeep, the motor of which was idling with Jean at the wheel, before the MP's caught up with us. We waited a short while until they were distracted by some people asking directions and then made a successful dash—the first leg of a nocturnal drop into France. Technically, I had gone AWOL from the hospital in order to get into action.

# CHAPTER 4

# Mission Jedburgh

Arriving at base, we packed our operational gear in our rucksacks which, with our carbines and ammo, were delivered to our packing shed at the airport at Blida, a suburb of Algiers. The gear would be packed in a bundle specially marked to be easily recognizable and dropped with all the other bundles and containers.

We had a short handshaking and backslapping session with a parting "good luck" from the remaining American and British Jeds and a *"merde"* from the French. In this case it had a connotation of good luck. But there were also congratulations for Henri and Jean who, respectively, had just been promoted to captain and lieutenant. My promotion to captain had been effected several weeks after our arrival in Algiers.

At the airport, we were put in security isolation at the Joe-house, where we stayed until takeoff time. Here a British officer briefed us on our mission in French for the benefit of Henri and Jean. Where I required a clarification, English would be used. Surprisingly, it was just that—brief. We were given reference maps of our area for the terrain and target review. Our attention was directed toward the railway, electrical, telecommunication, and highway systems. Our drop zone was indicated, as well as marine and industrial targets. The area was mainly the Gare and Lozère départements, but in certain sectors it extended to the Mediterranean coast. Our northern sector was mountainous and forested, good guerrilla country, in the Massif Central. In the south, it was flat and urbanized with towns and small cities that had various industries.

No time element restrictions were imposed on conducting operations except to prepare for maximum effort on receipt of the invasion alert. At the end of the briefing, we were each issued a silk map of southern France that we could wear as a scarf and an identical code book for enciphering and deciphering. Jean received the latest radio security instructions and checked out his call signs.

In the hems of my jump jacket and Henri's and Jean's trouser waistbands were sewn a small compass, a rubber-encased file, and some lock-picking equipment. We turned down an issue of cyanide pills, to use in case we were captured and threatened with torture, for fear we'd mix them up with quinine or aspirin tablets. However, we gladly accepted money belts bulging with thousands of francs.

After a light evening meal of cold sandwiches and hot cocoa, we were given the countersign to use on the drop zone. The waiting reception committee would ask us a question. "Qu'est-ce que l'homme porte?" And we were required to respond, "L'homme porte une veste à carreaux." This would signify that we were legitimate and not enemy agents attempting to infiltrate the guerrilla movement.

We still had some time to kill before our departure, which was around 2400—midnight. We spent it studying our terrain maps and finally gazing at magazines and discussing eventualities with which we would be faced.

At last, the briefing officer returned. We were driven to the plane, where he wished us "all the best," and slipped me a metal flask of cognac. We boarded, the engine revved up, and then, gathering speed, we rolled along the runway.

I always sweated out a takeoff. Once aloft, I'd feel great. We were off, but no lights were showing; the whole coast was blacked out. Crossing the Mediterranean, we noticed what looked like a shining jewel reflecting its rays through the blanket of darkness. The pilot, a British flight sergeant, told us it was the Balearic Islands of neutral

Spain. Then, after some minutes, we were enveloped once more in darkness, except for a dim light in the fuselage of the plane.

The jump master told us we were approaching the French coast and to hook up our parachute static lines. We snapped them on the plane's cable and he slapped us on the back to signify he'd rechecked. I passed the flask around and we all took a good swig. We looked and waited for the red light. The jump hole was small; only one man could sit on its edge at a time.

"You're number one," said the jump master pointing to me. He then indicated Henri as number two and Jean as number three. We tightened up our pistol belts and then the red light suddenly gleamed. I sat at the edge of the hole with my legs dangling in it. Henri and Jean were sitting sideways around the rim of the hole, ready to swing their legs into it.

The red light turned green.

"One, Go!" yelled the jump master.

I pushed off in the body position of attention. The prop blast hit as I exited and, after a few seconds, I felt the shock of my chute opening. I pulled on the risers to guide me toward the reception committee's three lights shining below.

Suddenly the lights were extinguished. Evidently the plane had dropped its load without making a second pass and was heading home. There was no target spot as a guide, so I just relaxed and drifted in the dark. Then my feet hit the ground and I rolled and banged my head on a rock. The helmet saved me from any abrasion, but the wallop hurt and befuddled me.

Gradually, the repetition of "Qu'est-ce que l'homme porte?" brought me around and, instead of continuing "Goddamn, what hit me?" I burst forth with the required response. Staring into the muzzles of a batch of Sten guns made my response more vociferous.

The security element guided Henri and Jean to our location. The Resistance chief and a few guerrilla leaders were there to receive and welcome us. They advised me that we'd get a briefing in a safe house nearby, but before we got started loud curses and the sound of scuffling pierced the air.

We rushed to the scene of the commotion and found a group of guerrillas scrapping over the contents of a busted bundle—mainly boots. I told the guerrilla leader whose units were handling the drop and for whom it was designated and to have them pipe down and settle the fracas.

This was the first warning I had on the quality of guerrilla security. I decided we'd wait until our special bundle was found. I wanted our carbines, Bren gun, ammo, and above all the suitcase radio and hand generator.

There was a truck *(gazogène)*, propelled by combustible gas produced by a charcoal-burning boiler, hidden under the trees close to a road. Our bundle, which had finally been found, was loaded onto it and with the help of a flashlight we retrieved the carbine, boxed ammo, and pouches of loaded magazines. Henri had Jean stay with the weapons and our personal equipment as well as the small cannister containing our radio equipment.

At a local farmhouse, the Resistance chief, who called himself Commandant Raymond, clued us in on the situation in the area. Then we sat around and were served a very late supper, which was delicious compared to our usual fare. We washed down supper with the local vintage. This was a hint of the gourmet meals with which we frequently would be favored.

During the briefing, I learned that the commandant's organization had completed the actual resistance phase and was just entering the guerrilla stage.* It appeared that it was the commandant's intention to set up the guerrillas in groups of from fifty to one hundred men in quite close proximity to one another. Recruiting had started and some embryo groups had been formed. Arms and ammo were in short supply and consisted of the sportsman's variety. The com-

---

*The resistance phase consists of gaining the support of the population; in organizing; providing intelligence to our outside HQ; and in disrupting enemy activities through sabotage, subversion, propaganda, etc. It is covert activity. The guerrilla phase is the final expression of a successful resistance: overt, actual warfare.

mandant had organized a supply system to feed his guerrillas and the resistance networks were operating in the urban sector. According to him, the escape and evasion network was rescuing a fair number of Allied pilots and filtering them into Spain. The network also indicated the location of the enemy forces.

No guerrilla action had yet been effected, but the commandant was anxious to start now that we had arrived. He realized we had the capability to furnish on a regular basis the arms and supplies to support guerrilla activity. He had received a few supply drops through a two-man SOE team in the general area that was primarily concerned with restraining any guerrilla activity until D day. This was called for in *Plan Vert,* but I had not been advised of it in my briefing at Blida Joe-house. These supplies were just a drop in the bucket compared to what would be needed. Commandant Raymond was careful to stipulate that he would commence operations only if we had no objections.

I announced that we were representatives of SHAEF, the Supreme Headquarters, Allied Expeditionary Force, and showed Raymond a document attesting thereto by General Koenig, Chief of the FFI, to which he owed his allegiance. Raymond was impressed and said he was ready to cooperate. I had questions in mind, but I figured I'd find the answers to most of them after checking out Raymond's organization. My gut feeling was that he'd either forgotten to include some things I ought to know or that he was reluctant at this time to divulge everything.

I was anxious to be off to the location Raymond had selected and recommended for our command post (CP) and so indicated. "Alors, il nous faut aller au Poste de Commandement que vous m'avez recommandé, près d'Alès."

Shortly before daylight, the truck was fully loaded and supposedly all the chutes had been buried. The concern over the chutes was due to the fact that, if they remained in the hands of the Maquis, the cloth eventually would be given to their wives or girl friends, who would make dresses or lingerie out of it. This posed the danger of being reported to the Gestapo by collaborators. The commandant and one of the guerrilla leaders would accompany us in the truck to a command post near a small village in the mountains further south and closer to Alès, the center of our area. The drop zone where we were was close to Mende in our northern sector.

The commandant and guerrilla leader were in the cab and we were lying under a tarpaulin that covered all the bundles and containers. Since the road ran from Alès in the south to a number of small villages in the upper reaches of the Massif Central—a fruit, grain, and vegetable farming area—the road was patrolled only intermittently by the Germans. It was considered relatively safe, although still we were tempting fate. However, the three of us, with Raymond and the driver, were well armed. I had gotten the British Bren gun out of the arms bundle and that could raise hell with a small patrol.

Not long after daybreak, we approached a village. Peering through an opening in the tarpaulin, I noticed something strange. A crowd was lined up in the street.

"Henri, il y a quelque chose très étrange dehors. Une foule est dans la rue."

The truck stopped and I heard people shouting. "Où sont les Américains?"

Since the cat was out of the bag and our infiltration was no longer a secret, I nudged Henri and Jean to get up. We pulled aside the tarpaulin, jumped up, and waved. An arm band of an American flag had been sewn on my right sleeve and when that became visible the crowd roared and started throwing flowers. Young women climbed up, with our willing assistance, to bestow kisses.

Either the news of our arrival had been leaked to spur recruiting or someone with a big mouth had confided in his wife or friends. Whichever, it was a gross violation of security since even our route had been disclosed.

With "Vive les Américains" ringing in our ears and the tarpaulin covering us again, we continued on our journey, repeatedly experiencing the same reception at a number of villages. At one village that hadn't received the word, the driver parked the truck behind a café and we entered through the back door. On noticing our uniforms, the proprietor rushed over, greeted all of us, and gave us a secluded table.

He had a special meal prepared and served champagne which he personally poured.

But we were not to enjoy seclusion for long. The place started filling up; people were flocking in and it was "Vive les Américains" once again. Everyone toasted us and wanted to touch our glasses, which resulted in a wine-soaked tablecloth and splotched uniforms. Suddenly the crowd became aware that Henri and Jean were in French uniforms and were French and the litany became "Vive la France!"

The show was on the proprietor. He wouldn't accept payment; we were his guests. Finally, feeling a bit high and with an invitation to drop in any time, we went out to the truck and were again besieged by the crowd. We climbed into the truck with a bit of difficulty. Commandant Raymond laughed; he was having a ball sporting around the representatives of the Supreme Allied Command.

We pushed off and before long Henri, who was in his cups, started taking potshots at any rabbit dashing across the road. Jean was snoring. I figured it was a lost day, one to forget.

But I did stop Henri's wasting of ammunition. "Gardez les cartouches pour les Boches," I reproached him.

By nightfall, we reached the village nearest the location of our intended command post. The commandant told the driver to hide the truck in a barn nearby. But first we unloaded the radio. The commandant took us to the house of a friend of his where we'd all stay. Raymond assured us that the guerrilla leader had arranged for security and that we'd be quite safe.

Nevertheless, I had Jean bunk the radio under a coal pile in the cellar and warned him that he should sleep in his underwear, with his boots on, and have his uniform and weapon handy. The same went for Henri.

Our room was on the ground floor. We no sooner hit the sack than we fell asleep. Sometime during the night, we were rudely awakened. The commandant was yelling, "Les Boches! Filez!"

We grabbed our uniforms and weapons, jumped out of the window, and followed the commandant along a trail running uphill into the forest. We could see vehicle headlights down below. My immediate concern was our radio. I hoped

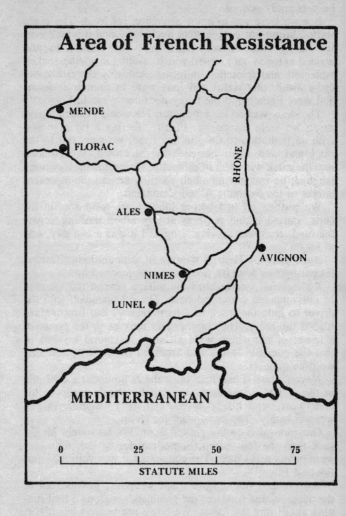

# Area of French Resistance

MENDE

FLORAC

RHONE

ALES

AVIGNON

NIMES

LUNEL

MEDITERRANEAN

| 0 | 25 | 50 | 75 |

STATUTE MILES

the Germans wouldn't find it. We'd forgotten we were garbed only in our underwear until Raymond quipped, "You're out of uniform."

The next day the guerrillas retrieved our radio. We had been lucky, since the only house that was searched was the one we slept in and still the radio had not been found. I discussed this with the commandant and gave him some ideas on how to ferret out the informer. There was no doubt that the organization was infiltrated by a confidant of his.

We moved our command post (CP) to an isolated farm. To obtain some semblance of security, I arranged a rendez-vous point with the commandant but left him in the dark as to the location of our CP, which we kept shifting.

In order to make a reconnaissance of the area and inspect the guerrilla groups (Maquis) that were already formed, we needed transportation. The commandant claimed he could purchase on the black market a serviceable motorcycle with two seats as well as a supply of gas for a few thousand francs. We also needed civilian clothes. All included, as well as I can recall, it amounted to 20–25,000 francs. We dished out the money and in a couple of days we were equipped.

We left Jean with the team equipment at the CP. Carrying our .45 pistols in shoulder holsters concealed under our civilian jackets, we started out with the commandant, who also rode a motorcycle.

In between visiting the various Maquis, we surreptitiously checked most of the major targets and the terrain in general. But the priority area was the Rhône Valley, which was our eastern boundary. Here were all types of targets combined. We met all the Maquis leaders and had a chance to evaluate them roughly.

On completion of the survey, I asked the commandant to call a meeting of his Maquis chiefs, which he did. I gave them my critique, stressing that more dispersion of the groups would offer better security and be less of a burden on the local communities furnishing food and other required supplies. I also recommended that a training program was needed in guerrilla tactics and sabotage and that groups should not be organized in strengths of more than thirty or forty men.

In order to speed preliminary preparations, I had Henri

start reorganizing the resistance networks using the network chiefs. He arranged for their training while I set up the guerrilla training. The main objective for Henri in this regard was to separate the intelligence and sabotage operations. Currently, one network was doing both as opportunities presented themselves. Since most sabotage targets are under guard, saboteurs are much more exposed to getting shot or captured than purely intelligence operatives. Therefore, not only sabotage but also intelligence operations could be compromised.

To facilitate the operation, a front-wheel drive Citroën had been requisitioned from a collaborator. With it was furnished a chauffeur/bodyguard, who was a Parisian and spoke fluent English. He came from a well-to-do family and had studied in England. He was in his mid-twenties, had an attractive and charming wife, and wanted to pull his weight in the Résistance. He became a member of our team and turned out to meet all of my expectations. He was *un débrouillard,* an operator. His nom de guerre was Michel.

I selected several training areas and took the Maquis leaders and their lieutenants for training. They were all ex-Army and required training just in guerrilla tactics; sabotage including the use of explosives; and familiarization with the U.S. carbine and 30-caliber machine gun, the Bren gun, Lee Enfield rifle, German Mauser, and Schmeisser submachine gun. Since even the bazooka was in short supply for regular forces, we had access only to the British *Pioneer Infantry Anti-Tank* (PIAT). It was a fearful weapon to fire, with the kick of a mule. You had to lie prone and even then it would kick you back a foot or so and favor you with a black-and-blue shoulder. After witnessing me fire a round, the guerrilla leaders swore off. They didn't want any part of it.

Upon completing this short, compact course, the leaders returned to their Maquis groups and started training them. As this went on, Michel drove me from one Maquis to another so I could demonstrate the different weapons and explosives and check on the guerrillas' progress.

In the meantime, a few drops (parachutages) had been effected and weapons, ammo, and explosives were being issued. And Henri secured the reorganization of the networks on the well-compartmentalized cell system.

Then we had the cell couriers and network chiefs report for training, which primarily concerned the sabotage net. I conducted the training and made the couriers responsible for training their cells and supplying them with plastic explosives, primer cord, detonators, fuses, and explosive gadgets.

However, during this period no guerrilla activity was permitted and only the intelligence, escape and evasion, and security nets were operational. I explained to Commandant Raymond that the organization should be trained properly and achieve reasonable strength before we started needling the enemy. But of course it would not be at maximum capability, except for the currently operating networks, until we got the invasion signal.

In discussing maximum capability, it was understood that the Maquis now being formed were to be cadres. We couldn't arm, supply, and maintain large forces under present circumstances. Airdrops were conducted only at night, usually during the full-moon periods. Thus, there was a severe limitation, logistically. This was somewhat alleviated by effecting a number of drops per night during the parachutage periods. The entire parachutage limitations would be lifted as D day approached so that the Maquis could support their enlargement. At this time, however, without an invasion to deter the Germans from conducting full-scale antiguerrilla operations, a large force, poorly armed, would make a suitable and vulnerable target. We would be courting destruction and disaster to the resistance movement in the entire sector.

The solution was for each Maquis to recruit personnel, whom they would train on a one- or two-day-a-week basis. The Maquis would establish a mobilization area for the new personnel, set up arms caches for them, and, on receipt of the invasion alert, mobilize them. These dormant guerrillas were called the Légaux.

Developing the reserve Légaux would not be a difficult task. Plenty of the men inhabiting our two departments had wanted to participate in the Resistance, but they had economic and family responsibilities and problems that had prevented them from serving. However, once the invasion was on, they'd flock to the Maquis. There was also additional ready manpower available. While southern France had been the unoccupied zone, hundreds of young men had taken refuge in our mountain areas to avoid being picked up and shipped to Germany as slave laborers by the dreaded *Service de Travail Obligatoire* (STO). This element couldn't be maintained in the Maquis presently, but they'd be eager to be on tap as reserves.

Raymond indicated that he had heard the Maquis in other départements were organized on more or less the same model but to such a degree that they were practically dormant, with their active Maquisards actually camping out and remaining inactive.

We agreed that all we just discussed could be accomplished at the same time we could be conducting limited action against the Germans, enough to keep them harassed.

To reinforce this rationale, I pointed out that keeping the Maquis inactive with nothing to do but a bit of training and attending to their camping chores would lead to boredom, laziness, lack of resolve, discouragement, and loss of morale.

Raymond then admitted that the Francs-Tireurs Partisans (FTP), a Communist-controlled national resistance movement totally independent of the FFI, was conducting continual and vigorous operations against the Germans. The FTP had a large nonactive following, many of whom were not communists. This paradoxical situation existed just because the FTP was combating the enemy aggressively. However, ex-military personnel in most cases refrained from tying in with them.

"Raymond," I asked, "would those individuals switch their allegiance and support to us if we started operations?"

"I'm sure that as soon as the word got around that we were in action, they'd rally to us."

"All the more reason for us to get cracking," I declared. "Our active Maquis are at reasonable strength and our armament is adequate. And the Légaux are sufficiently trained for limited operations. Why not make the effort now to get our Maquis operating, but not on any all-out basis?"

"Entendu! Je suis tout à fait en accord," Raymond responded in total agreement.

"And don't forget, it will force the Boches to increase

the size of their security forces and alert them to the necessity of assigning larger security elements along their withdrawal route during the invasion period. This will cause a reduction in their planned coastal defense force.'' I mentioned this expressly to assuage any doubt Raymond had of not hewing to the full requirements of *Plan Vert* and to give him a cogent reason and justification for such action. Therefore, although our major mission was to support the projected Mediterranean invasion by conducting limited operations now, we would temporarily be assisting the Normandy invasion. This would be a by-product of our local efforts to maintain the morale of the Maquis and the support and allegiance of the population.

Jean closely followed the BBC nightly radio broadcasts and, when we were not at our CP, kept us fully informed.

These broadcasts were a shot in the arm, not only for us and all the members of the resistance/guerrilla forces, but also for the vast supportive population. Regardless of the edict forbidding the possession of a radio, everybody was tuned in. Although at this period the progress of the Normandy invasion forces was slow and labored, they definitely had a sure footing in northern France.

According to Raymond, the supply and troop traffic northward through our area by road and rail exceeded that of the preinvasion period. This was another factor that influenced me to urge Raymond to get cracking on initiating at least limited operations. By that I meant using all his current active forces but still keeping the Légaux dormant.

Operations were to concentrate where the heaviest traffic flow existed—the Rhône Valley. Priority was to be given to conducting ambushes and disrupting the road and rail system in order to harass the traffic flow, which evidently was still assisting, in terms of troops and supplies, in reinforcing the forces resisting the Normandy assault.

Henri, Raymond, and I toured the area and I requested additional airdrops from our base in Algiers. We checked the activities of the groups and furnished them the latest tactical information obtained from our intelligence network. We participated in some of the ambushes, but we let the group leaders conduct the operations, furnishing advice when necessary. Where there was a special sabotage job to be handled, I'd advise the groups on the application of the demolitions, often combining plastic and incendiary charges for more effect.

The big task was to get the guerrilla leaders to make their ambushes short and furious—hit and run—and to watch their flanks while the action was underway. They were to withdraw into their mountain areas after an action while another group in another small sector would cover the valley. This would give the enemy security forces a fit as they tried to figure out where we'd strike next.

Since the Rhône Valley was a hot spot, convoys started coming through on the rails and road going from Alès to Clermont-Ferrand and further north. This was our mountain area.

Raymond quickly had some of the groups concentrated on this route and the traffic petered out. But road movement continued to be heavy at intervals in the valley.

Traveling on that inner road was a bit risky when it became an alternate route for the enemy, but we had to get around. In addition to Michel, who always drove, we had a hard-boiled, ex–foreign legion sergeant for additional security. He'd sit in the rear of the vehicle with a Bren gun. The rear window had been removed to facilitate firing from there if we were pursued. Raymond was usually with us carrying a Schmeisser submachine gun.

We were salvaging quite a supply of Mausers and Schmeissers. The units were warned to separate the ammo carefully for the different types of weapons that were being collected from small ambushes and that were contained in airdrops.

One day we were flagged down by one of our groups that had tapped the telephone line running alongside the inner road. They had been alerted that a convoy of about twenty vehicles was heading in their direction—northward.

Michel swung the vehicle up a dirt road bordered by trees. We stopped and unloaded some gammon grenades, each filled with about two pounds of plastic with a ball type of fuse and detonator that exploded on impact. The sergeant—François—with his Bren gun and the rest of us followed the guide while Michel parked the car some distance away off the dirt road under some trees.

The group leader showed us his deployed group in position. They were on an embankment with a good field of fire. The team that would stop the lead vehicle was posted on the right flank on a spur that jutted out onto the road, creating a small curve around which the road continued. From the spur the three-man team had a zone of enfilade fire in the direction from which the convoy would approach. The three-man security element on the left flank had a good zone of fire with a 30-caliber machine gun in case the enemy had any ideas of outflanking us.

As Raymond complimented the leader on his group's tactics, an incident occurred which I had foreseen but which I had never been told how to handle at Milton Hall.

A couple of peasants suddenly appeared to our rear as they took a shortcut to the highway. Were they to be trusted or would they warn the enemy? Raymond reacted instantly. He signaled the leader to have a man detain them, get them under cover, and keep them under guard until the ambush was over. In this case, Raymond gambled that the peasants didn't recognize any of the group. I was interested in the final solution—what to do with them if they did recognize anyone. The answers to that were varied, but rarely were severe measures taken unless the suspect was a known collaborator.

In the meantime, I had told François to support the right flank with his Bren gun. He jumped to it with glee. Two of the other three men each had been given a gammon grenade with which to stop the lead vehicle.

We'd been waiting quite a while and started thinking the alert was a false alarm when the left flank signaled that the convoy was approaching.

The commandant was with the group leader a bit higher up around the center of the ambush area, with a view to both flanks. Henri and I took up positions on the right flank spur, with a view of the length of the road. I reminded him and François that we would reassemble at our vehicle. Michel had been instructed to keep our Citroën close to the dirt road after the firing stopped and be prepared to take us along the side road deeper into the hills away from the through road.

As the lead vehicle reached the spur and started to circle

it, the first gammon grenade was thrown. It hit the road right alongside the front end, exploded, blew off the engine hood, and caused the vehicle to swerve toward the center of the road and stop dead. Just then, the second gammon hit the driver's compartment and a fire started.

Then all hell broke loose as the group opened up with rapid fire. I could hear François firing the Bren in bursts. From the spur, we were firing right down either side of the halted convoy.

Troops spilled out of the foremost and rearward trucks; the rest were loaded with supplies. It was hopeless for them to stay behind the trucks opposite our main body because we sprayed that area from the spur. To run away, they'd have to cross an empty field. The convoy commander sized up the situation, after taking some heavy losses in the first couple of minutes, and raced his men away from the spur toward our left flank to get around us.

That was when we heard the 30-caliber machine gun rattling away, which was also the withdrawal signal.

"Allons-y!" I yelled to François and Henri. The firing stopped, except for a few bursts now and then by our machine gunner, as we all dashed to the rear, away from the scene. The group raced for their reassembly area and we for our vehicle.

Michel was waiting for us, engine running and car facing in the desired direction. We sped off and, by a circuitous route, approached our command post, leaving Raymond out at a safe house where we usually rendezvoused.

"Merveilleux! Formidable! Une victoire!" Raymond placed the enemy casualties at fantastic numbers. If he spread that news around, it would be powerful propaganda. While he was describing the encounter to impress Michel, who appeared to be swallowing it all, in between the *formidables* Michel would throw me a wink.

After Raymond left, Michel grinned. "The commandant's gone nuts. I know he's just full of it. What was the enemy casualty count anyway?"

I asked Henri what he thought. He came up with a figure somewhat smaller than Raymond's and so did François.

"I'd say there were around one hundred and fifty enemy that tumbled out of the trucks and it appeared that at least fifty of those were casualties,'' Henri estimated. ''Plus a dozen or more remained in the vehicles. A reasonable total would be a minimum of sixty with a possibility of seventy. There definitely were more than twenty vehicles in that convoy.''

When we were examining the radio messages Jean had received and preparing answers with the latest information the Intelligence net had reported, Henri asked me to send a commendation for the group leader of the ambush. I was happy to accommodate and sent in a short squib using his nom de guerre.

By the early part of July, the military traffic by rail and road died down to normal. No more reinforcements to the German armies in Normandy and Brittany were forthcoming. And from the reports of our intelligence network, it appeared that the current enemy forces were preparing to resist a Mediterranean invasion.

Raymond was keeping the guerrilla activity low key. Our plan was to keep the enemy concerned over our routes of communication so that they'd have to maintain larger rear area security forces, thereby reducing their coastal defense forces.

However, the networks were operating at a level that was pinching the enemy. Sabotage, Intelligence collection, and escape and evasion were being conducted at a very active level. And the security net continually was ferreting out collaborators.

Now that the enemy reinforcing activity was over, Raymond had time to turn his attention to us. Large sweeps were being conducted in our mountainous guerrilla area, but not with any success. We always had good advance warning and our well-dispersed groups would just fade away. The enemy never came to grips with us and we adhered to our maxims: No set battles; no lengthy firefights; hit and run; keep dispersed.

The Germans became frustrated because they couldn't run us down. So they resorted to some nasty procedures. After an ambush, they'd dispatch troops to the nearest town, seize a dozen or so males off the streets, and summarily execute them. If we'd run an ambush midway between two towns, they'd repeat the procedure in each town.

This created problems for Raymond, since some of the mayors got after him to quit the cops-and-robbers activity. Innocent citizens were suffering because of it. It took Henri to settle this political problem that was really his responsibility anyway.

Henri listened to the complaints and then notified the mayors that sacrifices had to be made if they wanted France liberated. He informed them that we, La Résistance, had the full support of the population. We would be considerate, but we'd not reduce the activities we considered necessary.

The Gestapo in the towns and cities intensified their security measures. They attempted to increase their informant nets with a view to infiltrating our organization. But this was countered by our security net, which was hunting and eliminating collaborators.

The sabotage net in the urban sectors and the guerrillas in the rural area were conducting sabotage around the clock. The railroad track system, highways, telecommunications, and electrical systems were under siege. Marine sabotage was conducted in ports on the coast. Industrial sabotage, both passive and active, was underway. Workers in plants and factories producing supplies for the enemy were malingering and ruining machinery, shorting electric circuits, and intermittently cutting off electric energy by blasting the pylons supporting high-tension wires or blowing up the transformers. Locomotives were being damaged or rendered inactive through the introduction of simulated coal, made of plastic explosives, into the coal tenders and by blowing out turntables.

The Gestapo had a fit. Although they would pick up one of our agents or a cell now and then, it always ended there because of Henri's insistence that each cell be compartmentalized.

The Gestapo ran innumerable street spot checks. Everyone rounded up who didn't have a local *carte d'identité* would be handled initially as a suspect.

Since Henri and I had not been furnished such a document at the Joe-house, we carried one that had been obtained for us by Raymond. But it was a fake and could be spotted, particularly if a member of the *milice* was on hand. They were a French auxiliary police/security force operating for the Germans in a distinctive black uniform or in civvies. They were a nasty, vicious element convinced that the Nazis would remain masters of France and that they would be properly rewarded for their wartime service.

This situation made us a bit uncomfortable. We were usually in uniform in the guerrilla area, but when we were conducting a reconnaissance or other clandestine mission in the towns or cities we'd be in civvies. Luckily, most checkpoints were manned by Germans who didn't even understand French. However, there was always the threat of a first time.

Raymond and I, always driven by Michel and accompanied by François, kept touring the area, checking on the additional guerrilla groups being organized, always stressing dispersion and constant training. Not too frequently, we'd have to burst through a roadblock. For short distances, at times we'd resort to bicycles, but this wasn't often.

On these inspection and reconnaissance tours, we'd eat at various cafés in the villages and always received the usual welcome greetings, best dishes, and wines. We constantly were fêted. But still, we'd never get a bill. Raymond assured me that it was not an imposition. The proprietors considered it an honor.

Nevertheless, Michel claimed, "One day you'll pay and then through the nose!"

I also wondered when those gustatory welcomes would start wearing thin.

By this time the security net had trapped the collaborator, a former confidant of Raymond, who had informed on us upon our arrival. Through him, after some bruising interrogation, it was disclosed that the Gestapo had built up a dossier on Henri and me. We were classed as the leading terrorists in the area. We weren't sure if we should be proud of that dubious distinction. To the enemy we were terrorists, but to the local population and the army we were liberators. Raymond was categorized as a resistance leader but not as a terrorist, which sort of deflated him.

But we cheered him up. "Vous n'êtes pas le chef de la résistance, mais le grand chef!"

One day, Henri recommended that I commend the leader of an intelligence cell that was producing excellent coverage of coastal defenses. We met at a café in a town near Nîmes, where he operated some brothels for the German officer corps.

I congratulated him and he beamed.

"Merci! Je veux toujours faire de mon mieux. Jai une nouvelle idée!" He was going to import a batch of prostitutes, *poules,* with venereal disease. While plying their trade and unobtrusively pumping their Nazi clients for information, they would produce a bonus at the same time. They'd infect them!

The fact that he had been commended for his efforts to liberate his country evidently gave him a feeling of respectability which, he thought, raised him out of the filthy category of a pimp. Therefore, he assumed this new social attitude and offhandedly, as an aside, informed us that whenever we were in the neighborhood we'd be welcome—on the house!

"Pas de blague?" I said. "No kidding!"

Henri yanked him back to reality. "One case of VD from your establishments and you'll be a target for a German firing squad. Nous voulons des renseignments, pas des espions morts!"

After he departed, Henri and Michel called a spade a spade. "Il est un salaud!" But, we agreed, we needed the louse.

Although the Gestapo had picked up a few of our people, they didn't retain all of them. As soon as we would get news of someone's capture, all the networks would be alerted to ascertain where they were being held. Then Raymond would alert the security net to determine the most feasible method of obtaining their release.

If the detainees were in the hands of the French police, contact with the proper official often would develop a plan whereby the finger couldn't be pointed at that official. Bribery helped! If the detainee was in the custody of the Gestapo, a raid was required. This would be conducted by a local guerrilla group in coordination with the security net.

The reconnaissance of the building, guard system, and schedule of prisoner transportation would be effected by the selected agents of the security network in conjunction with the guerrilla leader involved. Based on the reconnaissance and adhering to the raiding tactics employed by our organization, the raid would be effected. When appropriate, the rescue attempt would be made while the prisoner was in transit. But that required very specific information.

We were not always successful, but when possible and feasible the rescue was attempted. To all of us, capture meant torture usually followed by elimination either during the torture stage or by firing squad or in a concentration camp gas chamber. Therefore, our rescue policy was twofold: to effect a release and to demonstrate that, whenever possible, a rescue attempt would be made. This sustained our morale and fortified us to take calculated risks.

Our activity against the enemy was now being conducted at a reduced scale, since the general situation was still fairly quiet and because I had been signaled to do so until the invasion was launched.

However, enough was happening to create casualties. They were light, but better medical assistance was required. There was also a morale factor. The individual guerrilla would perform his battle duties with more ardor and spirit and accept more risks if he knew that there was medical support in case he became a casualty.

Initially, casualties were treated by local doctors in their own clinic or a hospital. However, to obtain this service a casualty had to be transported, usually through well-populated urban areas, where these facilities were located, and where street spot checks were intermittently conducted. Also clinics and hospitals were under Gestapo surveillance and their informants were active in these facilities. This created an undesirable situation.

I discussed this with Henri and Raymond with the result that a medical network was added to our clandestine operations. Safe houses—usually barns—were set up as rudimentary hospitals. Doctors and nurses were recruited to staff them, aided by local volunteers, mostly women, to handle the housekeeping chores. Jean made urgent radio requests for essential medical supplies. With these special items in our airdrops, a reasonable supply was gradually collected. This service was publicized to all the guerrilla groups and to the networks. The leaders and couriers reported a definite lift in morale when the word got around. I visited a few of these small installations and, although not to be compared to military base hospitals, they were adequate for all but the most serious cases.

We still hadn't received any bazookas. But some British two-inch mortars had been dropped to us with both smoke and high explosive rounds. I ran a special training session for the group leaders on this type of mortar and warned them that the green-colored shells were smoke and the yellow were high explosive. I stressed that they should get rid of the smoke rounds.

On a subsequent ambush, the group leader confided that he was going to try out his mortar section. I advised him to have his forces deployed further from the road in case of a short round. This he did, moving his men further up the slight embankment.

Shortly thereafter, a fairly large convoy came barreling down the road. The lead vehicle was stopped with a couple of gammon grenades and rapid fire ensued. The enemy troops piled out of the trucks, got behind them, and built up a base of fire.

Then I heard the mortars and saw the rounds hit the vehicles. But instead of producing casualties and setting vehicles afire, a pall of dense smoke started spreading over the convoy, obliterating it. The leader gave the withdrawal signal and we bugged out to the rear into the forest.

On parting, the leader, red in the face with humiliation, since I had witnessed his good ambush being botched, was repeatedly calling his mortar section chief *"un salaud"*— "son of a bitch."

In another ambush situation, we were at a vantage point with the group leader. The enemy started a flanking movement around our left flank after a few minutes of action. The leader had a small, flank-protection detail posted to prevent and/or signal such an attempt. But the U.S. 30-caliber light machine gun bursts failed to materialize. Fortunately, the situation was visible from our vantage point and the withdrawal was signaled by the leader.

At the reassembly point, I asked the machine gunner to show me some of the rounds in the ammo belt. It was then that the teachings of the Scottish major came in handy. I felt the cartridges and then looked at them. They were Mauser rounds for the German rifle. The gunner had been careless and mixed them in with the U.S. 30-caliber batch. Naturally, the weapon wouldn't fire. The gunner had been under the impression that the weapon was malfunctioning. When I had him extract the rounds from the belt and reload with the correct ammo, the weapon immediately fired. I don't think that luckless chap ever forgot the difference between those cartridges. No doubt, the major's way of learning was the best: learn before you go into action rather than on the job.

This was not the only instance concerned with mixed-up ammunition. We had so many different weapons with as many different sorts of ammunition that unless we adhered to strict control measures, these incidents would occur. And they continually did, regardless of my exhortations.

One night, on a drop zone north of Alès around the northern boundary of our area, Henri and I were witnessing a night drop. We were with the group leader for whom the drop was intended. The drop had just been effected and the flashlights had been extinguished when a band of intruders suddenly appeared with their Sten guns aimed at us.

It was a stickup, not for our personal valuables but for something more desirable—the bundles and containers that were strewn over the drop zone. The intruders had disarmed the group's security element and scattered the labor team that was supposed to gather and load the dropped cargo. Our group leader recognized our assailants as the top leaders of a Communist group that operated south of our area and, at times, within it, as it suited them. They belonged to the Francs-Tireurs Partisans (FTP), a national communist resistance/guerrilla movement. They did not cooperate or operate in conjunction with the FFI, our organization. Neither did they enjoy the supply and financial support of the Supreme Allied Command. Therefore, it wasn't above the Communist group leaders to highjack a supply drop. They had some active elements in our area around Nîmes, Alàs, and a few other industrial areas, but had no following in the rural areas. They were in action from time to time, but appeared to be holding back and saving their powder for more devious politically oriented purposes.

The FFI were nationalists. Their goal was to drive out the German occupation forces and liberate France as a democracy, a new republic—the Fourth! The FTP were only concerned with gaining control of the government at every level as the enemy retreated in order to form a Communist France!

Since the FTP had the drop on us, there wasn't much we could do. They got the load but, strangely enough, it was the only such incident in our area.

We immediately reduced the number of drop zones in service. We redoubled the security elements of our reception committees and warned them of this internal new menace.

Time had been flying. We had been so occupied that we hadn't paid much attention to dates. But in early August, I noticed that the radio messages from Algiers were pressing more for specific coastal defense and order-of-battle information. In my opinion, something big was brewing—perhaps the Mediterranean invasion.

Based on that hunch, I reviewed our status with Henri and Raymond. Our Intelligence reports for some time had given quite broad coverage of the enemy situation: coastal fortifications and armament as well as troop unit designations and locations. All we could do was to have the Intelligence net redouble its efforts, to note any changes in previously reported positions, and to watch for any new additional emplacements.

In terms of organization, we were at what I considered maximum form as far as current active forces, communications, control, and especially logistics were concerned. The groups were still kept well dispersed, were well trained, and had been bloodied in action.

If my hunch was correct, we were on the verge of entering the final phase of a guerrilla campaign—the linkup phase. This would most likely propel us into a conventional military posture, requiring us to reorganize into companies and battalions—a true paramilitary unit. Of course, the size of our units would be smaller and more lightly armed than the conventional ones, since we had no heavy support weapons.

But we would be prepared to link up with advancing Allied forces and to support them.

I had Raymond alert his group leaders for such an eventuality for planning purposes without divulging that an invasion might be imminent. We did not want to take the risk of a security leak, although we realized that the Germans were fully aware of a projected invasion attempt.

Raymond started setting up a regimental staff and a simple but adequate Table of Organization. I figured that we had taken the necessary measures to prepare for whatever support would be required from us. Then we waited and stayed close to our command post, expecting the alert message that we had been briefed on back at the Joe-house. That seemed ages ago.

"C'est venu!" called Jean, "voilà le message." The imminent invasion alert had arrived. Jean decoded our special orders.

Our mission now was to keep the Germans in the Rhône Valley whenever their northerly retreat would occur. The purpose was twofold: to keep them from using secondary roads in the Massif to avoid deadly air strafing and, by forcing them to concentrate their retreating forces in the valley, afford the Air Corps concentrated troop targets. We then reorganized into a light paramilitary regiment of three battalions. Since practically all the guerrillas were ex-soldiers and officers, they were quite at home in this quasi-conventional formation.

Most of the roads leading into the mountains (the Massif) ran northward through Alès. Two battalions were posted to block off the roads in that vicinity. The other battalion was in a blocking position further north on another entrance route.

A few days after the alert message arrived, we heard naval gunfire which confirmed it. We had small reconnaissance units watching the main retreat route. When the retreat started to enter our sector, we were notified by motorcycle couriers and telephone.

Our command post was at the telephone exchange (the postal, telephone, and telegraph center) in Alès. This allowed us maximum use of the telephone system which we could utilize since the Gestapo, who had monitored the lines, was bugging out with the Army. Thus, our blocking battalions had ample advance notice whenever enemy units attempted to gain access to the mountains.

Over the period of the retreat, a number of the enemy units attempted to break through to the secondary mountain roads, but they'd always bounce off our positions and head back to the valley to suffer Air Corps strafing. But stragglers would manage to infiltrate and they had to be hunted down because they were starting to terrorize the farmers, particularly to obtain bicycles and food.

We handled this with roving, motorized patrols, since we now had a collection of vehicles from collaborators and salvaged German combat vehicles.

Not being able to resist the opportunity, we'd go off to *faire la chasse*—hunting for the Boche—and we'd blast them off the road or chase them into the woods. The ones that fought the fiercest, strangely enough, were Mongols and Tartars (formerly known as Cossacks). Among their Russian POW's, the Germans had recruited dissidents such as Mongols, Tartars, Ukrainians, and Muslims. These were organized into battalions for occupation duty in France.

On several occasions, we'd have these characters trapped in outbuildings, but they'd never surrender as the average German soldier was inclined to do. We'd have to kill them, which Henri, Michel, and François much preferred although they admitted that it was too bad they weren't Germans. "C'est dommage qu'ils ne soient pas des allemands."

One day at the Alès command post, I witnessed something unique. A report had just been received from our battalions holding the Alès road that an enemy unit had been repulsed and was heading back into the valley. The news spread around the city. Then, from being practically a closed shop, Alès underwent a metamorphosis. It blossomed into a city *en fête*. A holiday mood prevailed. Window shutters were pushed open, flags were unfurled, crowds burst into the streets, cafés poured wine, and the fire and police bands marched to the city hall square blasting forth *La Marseillaise*. A few hours later, a report was received that our battalions were under attack. This time the news got around with the opposite effect. Alès became a dead, besieged city again. This rotation of elation and gloom was displayed for at least the next three or four days like a faucet being turned on and off.

Right after the enemy retreat closed out of our sector, we were overrun by advance elements of the U.S. Seventh Army. We were then directed to mop up bypassed enemy units since the Seventh Army was in hot pursuit, intent on attempting to destroy the main body.

We then deployed into our southern urban sector, where enemy pockets were still holding out, and started liberating one town or city after another. It was in this final stage that we took most of our casualties, since quite a bit of bloody street fighting ensued—something I originally didn't visualize for guerrillas when Henri and I underwent the street-fighting course near London.

At this point, it became a race between us (FFI) and the Communists (FTP) to liberate communities. Whenever the FTP got to a municipality first, they took over the city hall; then they installed a Communist-controlled local government and left a control unit there to prevent any change.

Although tempted to evict these interlopers, Henri and Raymond decided to refrain from conducting a local civil war. We just concentrated on beating them to as many locales as possible. However, it was at Nîmes, famous for its ancient Roman arena, that we settled the drop-zone-stickup score with them.

The FTP had reached the city ahead of us and had taken over the city hall and booted out the local officials. A small Nîmes delegation contacted us and requested aid in restoring order and removing the FTP. At first, Raymond explained that shortly French units of the U.S. Seventh Army would rectify the situation. But the delegation insisted that we aid them immediately, since they represented the loyal citizens of the city. I was noncommittal, but Henri and Raymond knew that I had a hidden desire to even things up. An affirmative decision was rapidly made. It took a bit of time to gather up sufficient elements of our command and then we proceeded on the double.

We had directed the delegation to take off posthaste and have as large a crowd as possible in the city hall square around our expected time of arrival. We wanted the delegation to get the crowd pepped up and supportive of us.

At the outskirts of the city, our advance elements brushed aside a few FTP roadblocks and raced for the city hall with us and the main body closely behind. We underwent some sniping from rooftops which we considered symbolic. But it may have been intended in earnest since some of our more cocky stalwarts were sporting captured German helmets, items of uniform, and gear on their persons. However, this failed completely to hinder us in reaching the city hall, which our advance formation had already secured, although the Communist-installed representatives were still inside.

Raymond sent an aide in, holding up a white handkerchief, to deliver his offer to let the representatives leave in safety if there was no resistance. In the meantime, the crowd was alternately screaming "Vive la France" and "En bas les Communistes!" Realizing the dangerous mood of the crowd, which was on the verge of becoming an ugly mob, the FTP governing element quickly beat a retreat from the building, showered by boos, rocks, and bottles from the crowd.

The commandant headed for the mayor's office with us at his heels. The commandant then cooled off a bit and stepped out on the balcony. The crowd greeted him with an approving roar and, when they quieted down, he thanked them for their loyalty and cooperation. His address was short and to the point—the occupation was over!

And then the commandant put me on the spot. "Mon capitaine, quelques mots, s'il vous plaît."

Henri gently but firmly edged me out onto the balcony. When they saw me in a U.S. uniform with the Stars and Stripes on my right sleeve, the crowd went wild. Again I heard the rousing greeting, "Vive les Américains!" The continued cheering afforded me a few moments to gather my senses and, finally, I addressed the crowd with a few verbal gems. I thanked them for the courage they had shown in freeing their city, not only from the Boches but also from the threat posed by the Communist FTP. I wound up by calling them all Maquisards—the guerrilla element of La Résistance. Then we retired from the balcony with "vives" ringing in our ears. Through me, the U.S. was being praised by the citizens of Nîmes for its liberation role.

To me, this experience was the zenith of our mission. It

was the thrill of a lifetime! I've had a few since then, but none compare.

We were in a celebrating mood. Our responsibilities were about over. Raymond had reservations made at a favorite Nîmes restaurant. Quite a crowd assembled there that evening and, for once, Jean was along. The food reflected the excellence of Provençal cuisine and there were numerous toasts washed down with choice *vin du pays*—local wine.

I mentioned to Henri that this dinner was going to cost a bundle.

"Not at all! It will be on the house, as usual."

Michel overheard him. "This time we'll get hooked! Locally, the war is over!"

He wasn't wrong. The maître d'hôtel brought the bill directly to our table. Henri looked at it and silently passed it on to me. When I saw the digits comprising the sum, I burst out in wild laughter! I couldn't stop! That bill made up for all the free meals we'd had! I paid it willingly in spite of Raymond's protestations. It cleansed my conscience! All the generosity I had accepted from those grateful proprietors had made me feel like a moocher.

The dinner was over, it was still early, and we hadn't shaken off the celebrating mood. What next?

Almost in unison, Raymond and Henri burst forth. "Le salaud! Let's visit the girls of the cell that reported all that good intelligence."

The brothel owner's main establishment was in Nîmes and we had an open invitation. Michel drove us to a flashy section of the city where the bordello was located. Raymond's security detail followed. They would maintain guard over our vehicles which were loaded with our weapons.

We entered and asked for *le propriétaire*. The madame said he was out but that we were especially welcome. Raymond kissed her on both cheeks—a dignified, formal, initial approach—and told her we were accepting the proprietor's standing invitation and to break out the champagne. The girls trooped in and were congratulated for the dangerous service they had rendered their country.

"And for fattening their bankrolls!" Michel whispered to me.

It then became a ball, really a bash. The joint was ours.

Madame and the girls were elated to share the camaraderie of the leaders for whom they had worked so hard! The champagne kept flowing, the phonograph kept playing, and, between dancing and the drunken bragging of admired warriors, some of our group kept disappearing. Later they'd reappear, although with some difficulty in negotiating the stairs leading to the upstairs rooms.

I vaguely remember asking Michel, who didn't indulge in the festivities, "Where's Raymond?" or "Where's Henri?" since they seemed to fade away once in a while.

I seemed to hear, "They're here. You're getting them confused with our security guys who are taking turns wearing out the stairway carpeting."

Needless to say, we didn't get back to Alès, our command post, that night.

On leaving, I thinned out my money belt a bit more. "Madame, achetez quelque chose pour les girls."

When the *adieus* and the *bonnes chances* had been said, we departed.

En route, I asked Michel, "Did I disappear last night?"

"In the condition you were in, you couldn't have climbed those stairs, even with one pulling and another pushing."

I would have preferred a yes or no, but I didn't press him.

Realizing that my team would be recalled soon, I mentioned a few last items to Raymond. These included personnel to be recommended for decorations and rosters of all personnel of his organization, necessary for pay and promotion purposes. He assured me that his staff was working already on that project. He asked me what the future had in store for me and Henri. I replied that Henri most likely would continue his service with the French counterpart of OSS and that I personally would like a mission in Germany now that France was on the way to total liberation.

Henri and Michel suggested we take a trip to Cannes and Nice before we got orders to report at some OSS assembly base. However, I felt we did not have approval to leave our area until authorized. Then the inevitable occurred with the arrival of an OSS lieutenant colonel who ordered us to report to an OSS station in Grenoble.

We bade farewell to Raymond, his staff, and some of the

group leaders with whom we'd become familiar. François, to whom we'd become attached, almost had tears in his eyes when I gave him a last handshake.

The last remark I made to Raymond was "N'oubliez pas de recommender Michel et François pour une décoration."

Off we went in our Citroën with Michel at the wheel. His wife had agreed to spare him for the trip, since she wanted to return to Paris and he wanted to report there for regular duty. In return, I told him that as far as Henri and I were concerned he could keep the car—spoils of war.

We drove through Avignon and up the Rhône Valley and swung northeast to Grenoble. Upon arriving, Michel made me promise to look him up if I were ever in Paris. We sent our best wishes to his lovely wife and he took off.

There were about a dozen Jed teams at the small compound and we compared notes. The teams of course were dissolved and we were just a pool of operatives. There was nothing much to do except relax and wind down.

I requested the compound commander to notify London that I was ready for a mission in Germany. My German was fairly fluent, although not grammatically correct, and I had a good accent. Furthermore, I had traveled extensively in Germany and Austria.

All those who had been team leaders were asked to write a summation of their team accomplishments in terms of forces organized, drops, casualties inflicted on the enemy, and major actions. At the same time, about the third day after our arrival, a reply from London ordered me to report there forthwith.

I wrote a brief after-action report since I was now pressed for time and covered only a few highlights. An OSS plane would be taking off in a few hours. It later appeared that the more detailed, lengthy reports produced a more influential impact in many respects.

All the figures were approximate and were based on my personal observations, as well as Henri's and the reports Raymond had furnished. The result showed around three thousand effectives which included the trained and armed full-time guerrillas, Légaux and networks, and a few small Maquis groups not directly under Raymond's control. Also estimated was the rush of last-minute patriots who joined in after the invasion. Although they were not really trained and were skimpily armed, they helped to some extent. Enemy losses were around one thousand including prisoners, and there were around a dozen or more airdrops.

Then I took off for the airport, leaving a note for Henri saying that I would most likely see him in London.

On the flight to London, I pondered over the very brief report I had submitted. Admittedly, my team had not participated in the strictly resistance phase, but we did in the entire guerrilla phase from the organizational through the linkup stages. Therefore, we could not take credit for the total force developed, but certainly for a good percentage of it. Raymond and his leaders did the lion's share. But in the training and arming, plus the revitalization and final professionalism of the networks, we were in the fore.

However, it slowly dawned on me that our three-man team had obtained incredible results. Considering that a number of teams had been dropped in various areas, the total score for the Jedburghs must have run into six figures. A phantom army had struck and melted away repeatedly and had bled the enemy economically and militarily and had paralyzed its war effort right in the heart of the short-lived Nazi empire.

Had I performed well? I could have done better. I could recollect some circumstances and situations that could have been resolved more successfully. To appease myself, I chalked them up to inexperience—my first mission. Would the future afford me another chance? The fact that my request for a new mission had been responded to inflated my hopes for that opportunity. Would it be in Germany or perhaps Austria—somewhere in the Third Reich?

# CHAPTER 5

# Spinning Wheels

My meditations, which bordered on phantasies, ended when I was alerted that we were approaching London. The city was still visible in the evening twilight. With nightfall it would disappear, enveloped in its wartime blackout. I had my fingers crossed as usual when we came in for the landing. I exhaled as the plane bumpily touched down. I debarked and the gunner handed me my rucksack and carbine. A jeep was waiting and I was whisked to OSS headquarters in Grosvenor Square, located in the chic Mayfair area. It was only several blocks from Park Lane, the posh center of London's luxury hotels. The U.S. Embassy was on the square, close to the dignified, Georgian OSS building, which bore no sign of being the headquarters of a covert, clandestine organization which, of all things, was conducting guerrilla and resistance activities all over occupied Europe.

I reported to the duty officer. He checked his billeting roster and scratched his head. "We're really tight for quarters. What we've got tonight is pretty sorry."

I pointed to my waist. "I still have a fat money belt."

"In that case, why don't you live it up tonight and stay at one of the swanky hotels?"

"Swell! I'll leave my rucksack and carbine with you and try my luck."

First though, I rummaged through the rucksack and ex-

75

tracted my musette bag which contained clean underwear, socks, and toilet articles. Since .45's had a habit of disappearing, I kept my pistol in its holster hanging from my magazine-pouch-laden pistol belt. Swinging the musette bag over my head so it would hang in back from my shoulders, I departed for luxury, or at least a taste of it.

I first tried one of the swankiest hotels in the Mayfair section of central London. Attired in my dirty, stained jump uniform, musette bag on my back and my pistol butt bulging out of the top of its holster, I barged into the lobby. I did notice that, as I entered the foyer, the doorman, dressed like an admiral, gave me a funny look. The desk clerk appeared quite alarmed when I asked for a room and bath. People in the lobby, some in evening clothes, evidently attending some affair, looked askance at me. I started to feel uncomfortable. The clerk, with a superior air, looked past me and signaled to a burly individual.

When he approached, I said, "Not the house detective?" The clerk nodded. "We must request that you leave, sir. Civilian clothes or service uniform are de rigueur."

I was escorted out politely but firmly. One more attempt at another palatial establishment was made with the same, not-too-subtle result—the bum's rush. Since I was not de rigueur I figured I'd better lower my sights.

Finally, I wound up in a small but dignified hotel that Henri had turned down when I was entertaining him in London during the Milton Hall days. It hadn't been good enough for him then, the old devil, but it was definitely a notch better than sleeping in barns, haystacks, on the ground, and in vehicles. And there was a bonus—hot water for a bath!

The next morning I was back at OSS headquarters, clean underneath but with a dirty exterior. I turned in my weapons and field gear and retrieved my duffle bag and val-pack containing my de rigueur uniforms. Then I was assigned a billet in a rooming house. Before leaving, I was directed to turn in my operational funds to the finance officer. He required only a brief, rough accounting of funds disbursed. And that's exactly what it was, short and approximate. I had a lot of back pay to my credit and, now that I was fresh out of francs, I reloaded with a much smaller wad of pounds, thus restoring my waist to slimmer proportions.

On the way out, I stopped at the adjutant's desk and inquired if there were any orders or instructions for me.

"Report here daily. Let's see, I believe there is a message for you. The German desk wants to see you tomorrow." I left in high spirits, full of anticipation.

When I arrived at my quarters—a brownstone house in a street full of identical ones, row upon row of them off Baywater Road close to Marble Arch—the landlady, a very kind, motherly, middle-aged cockney, showed me to the door of my room. She informed me that another American was sharing the billet and she advised me that breakfast was served from 7 to 8 A.M. and that I should expect to be served oatmeal and prunes daily, with a supplement of scrambled powdered eggs on occasion, and toast and jam.

She evidently expected me to express disapproval of such a spartan gustatory regimen. But when I told her that I enjoyed such a high-fiber fare, she beamed and immediately advised me that I'd have a change of towels daily, evidently something reserved for star boarders only!

I knocked and walked in, deposited my luggage, and heard, "What the hell!" from across the room. It was my old buddy Bill. This was truly a happy coincidence.

While I unpacked and peeled off my well-worn uniform, Bill asked me if I had come back with another batch of Jeds.

"No, I left some at the compound in Grenoble, but I came alone."

"What happened to Henri and your radio operator?"

"I asked for a German mission and they rushed me back. Remember I'm almost as fluent in German as you are in French, although I'm deficient in grammar."

"Hope you click. I don't see much coming my way. The rumor is that China is the next theater for most of us."

We couldn't stop questioning one another.

"How long have you been back?" I asked.

"I was overrun early and I have been here more than three weeks sitting on my ass."

"Have you seen any of the gang around here?"

"Yes, they're around. You'll bump into them at the officers' mess, the Red Cross hostel, and the pubs."

"Tell me, Bill, did some of our fellows catch it?"

"So far, I understand that Larry Swank was accidentally

shot by one of his Maquisards. Seems the guy had his Sten gun cocked and when he stubbed his toe it went off. No medical aid was available and poor Larry bled to death.''

"What a hell of a way to die for such a decent chap!'' He had been a favorite with all of us and was one of our youngest, most promising officers.

"Bonsall paid the piper,'' continued Bill. "Got caught with his team and a few Maquisards moving weapons and their radio hidden under loads of hay in ox carts—summarily executed!''

There was nothing I could say. Some of our people were captured and were still being held. Among them was Cy, who'd been our commanding officer in the operational group. However, his luck still held out. He'd been caught by German troops, who, for some unknown reason, did not turn him over to the Gestapo.

All in all, our losses had been light, much lower than we had expected. Some of the British and French had been wounded and a few sustained jump injuries. The Dutch element suffered heavy losses supporting the Arnhem airborne assault. However, it appeared that the cards were stacked against the West-Pointers with Larry killed and Cy captured.

Bill didn't tell me much about his mission. He just gave me some of the highlights. The team had been dropped in Brittany, about fifty miles away from the designated drop zone. The area was crawling with Germans. The team could move only at night and finally had to spend most of their time hidden in the belfry of a church, which was made available due to the good graces of the curé. Bill participated in only one fierce firefight, although the team did manage to furnish some tactical intelligence to the heavily engaged U.S. forces, and a small Maquis that the team had finally collected offered some flank protection. But this phase occurred after they were overrun. Bill did experience a hair-raiser one night when the team's car was stopped by a German advance detail of a large, motorized column. Bill and his team leader, Major Jean-Paul, slid out and grabbed their pistols. But in the darkness, the enemy didn't notice their uniforms or .45's. All they wanted was to get the vehicle off the road so it would not interfere with the column's formation. The team obliged and continued its journey after the column passed.

Their mission was a glaring example of bad planning by headquarters: a top-notch team of extremely capable officers wasted in an area almost devoid of any guerrilla potential. Their briefing had been ridiculous—destroy around twenty bridges. With the Americans closing in on the area, the mission would have severely hampered logistics and Bill and Jean-Paul could have been responsible for some justifiably raving-mad commanders.

Bill's team leader, Jean-Paul, had been so frustrated and discouraged by the whole affair that he had requested duty with his regiment. His remark to Bill had been, "Je m'en fou de cette espèce de guerre!" He was fed up.

In one of my de rigueur uniforms, I accompanied Bill to a local pub frequented by a number of the Jeds. Over a variety of meat pies and greens, we chewed the fat with them, comparing notes and swapping tales. I also reacquainted myself with my favorite nectars, English ale and Guinness stout.

Unnoticed by us at first, a British officer with a crutch under one arm and one leg slightly bent at the knee with a cast on the lower portion was ordering a drink at the bar. When I happened to glance in that direction, I suddenly recognized the Milton Hall Romeo—Reggie!

I went over and grabbed him. "Come on over and join us. I'll bring your drink."

I swiped a chair from a nearby table and when he had settled himself I asked, "Now, what the hell happened to you? Not a victim to London traffic?" I said disparagingly but good-humoredly.

"Goddammit, this is a combat wound, you bastard," he laughingly retorted, patting his injured leg. But he didn't appear anxious to elaborate.

"Come on, Reggie, you can tell us, your old buddies. We'll keep it a secret," at which we all laughed.

Then sheepishly he admitted that his prime weakness, the natural urge for a female, had induced him to sneak into one of the towns in his operational area where he shacked up in a local brothel. The usual occurred. The Gestapo was tipped off and Reggie had to jump out of an upstairs bedroom, causing him to crack his ankle. Nevertheless, he was able to avoid capture.

"What the hell explanation did you give to get that injury into the combat category?"

"That you chaps will never know! But you can see that I sport the Mention in Dispatches, whereas all you blokes might have gotten would have been a Purple Heart!"

Sure enough, he was wearing the gold leaf insignia of that decoration—always the operator!

Bill and I finally broke away and took a brisk walk in Hyde Park. We were both a bit older than most of the Jeds and had experienced a much larger spectrum of life than any of them. To me, they were grownup kids, most of them just out of college. Regardless, some of them handled themselves outstandingly in dangerous and awkward situations that not only required courage but also good common sense, judgment, and savoir faire. They had learned, under duress and pressure, to cope with the vicissitudes of life at a much earlier age than we.

"What will their generation be like when they reach forty?" I posed to Bill.

"They'll be cynical, too damn sure of themselves, and hardboiled."

"Sophisticated, yes! But I'm not sure about the rest, Bill. You know, physically, I can still run the pants off a lot of them, if not in speed then definitely in distance. And don't forget, when they shipped all of us to that psychological testing center near Plymouth, didn't I break the record for climbing a rope up a tree and then pulling myself along the rope stretched between a brace of them? I can still remember how amazed the staff was when they asked me if I could have done better if I'd known I was being clocked and I said, 'Damn right, I could!' And they knew I wasn't kidding."

Bill laughed. "You've spent your lifetime training in long-distance swimming, wrestling, and gymnastics. They haven't had the opportunity or maybe the discipline to lead such a spartan existence. If they had, like some of them who were college athletes, you'd be outclassed."

"Hey you old bastard, you trying to take the wind out of

my sails? Come on, step on it, you've been sitting on your butt too long!''

Bill had deflated me. I was getting too cocky for my own good. I was underestimating the capabilities of others in order to boast my imagined invincibility. Of course any of those younger Jeds I'd been referring to who kept themselves in decent physical shape could take me on. This kind of overconfidence could have a bad impact operationally. Time to come down to earth!

After a couple of gin and tonics in a cozy pub, we dropped into the Dorchester House which had been requisitioned, either totally or partially, as an officers' mess, club, and temporary billet. We killed some time at the club, had dinner, and then hiked back to our quarters and hit the hay—a pattern that we often followed.

I reported to the German desk the next day. It was manned by a civilian in his late fifties—an academic type who had been a professor of German literature and history at some prestigious university when OSS enticed him.

He told me apologetically that the Allied advance had been so swift that the OSS hadn't had a real opportunity to do any advance planning for covert activities in Germany. But he buoyed my hopes when he said he'd have some rough mission outlines ready in about a week. Then, just as quickly, he partially deflated them. ''But they will be only Special Intelligence (SI) missions. We have no definite information on which to base a resistance/guerrilla operation.''

He indicated that SI recently had been able to insert only a few agents on shallow behind-the-lines missions. They were supplying just tactical stuff. The few long-term agents operating on a high espionage level were concerned with political factors.

I stressed that I much preferred a Special Operations (SO) task, since I belonged to that branch. However, I left the door open because I reasoned that the war in Europe wouldn't last much longer and I wanted a second chance.

I agreed to return in a week and went directly to the Special Operations branch. I discussed the matter with them and they were not too encouraging.

''No, we haven't gotten anything from the German desk

on which to base an SO mission. No information on dissident groups that have a guerrilla potential. Internal security, under the control of the Gestapo and the Abwehr, is tight as a drum in Germany," one of the staff informed me.

"And historically, such activity within that country has never occurred. They respect authority, whether it's that of a kaiser or a dictator," offered another.

"But how about Austria? Although it's part of the Third Reich, I'm sure much of the population is unhappy with their lot."

"The same security applies there, and again no factual information relating to your premise" was the answer.

The most I could get out of them was that they'd release me from SO for an SI mission if I'd request it.

"I'll let you know what I decide," I said, "but if something turns up, get hold of me."

They thanked me for my interest in stirring up an SO mission. Actually, they wanted to develop one to justify retaining their European pool of SO operatives. If Germany were out of the picture, even their declining operations in northern Italy would fold.

The week went by slowly. It dragged! I started up my exercise regimen in the backyard of our billet and this daily refresher killed some of the time. Dining at the officers' mess or snacking at the Red Cross helped, but pub hopping was the best tonic, fortified with ale or stout and dart throwing. And we did scout around central London and got to know every street and square and interesting shop.

I stopped by SO before reporting to the German desk.

"Nothing new. We want to use you, but there's still no intelligence on which to base anything."

"Keep trying. I'll be back!" and on I went to see my professor friend who held sway on the next floor.

He smiled as we shook hands. I hoped it was a good omen. "I've got a couple of tentative missions in which you might be interested. How about parachuting in the Bavarian Alps south of Munich near Bad Tölz? We know there is an officers' school there. You'd be impersonating a German sergeant and your mission would be to filch documents from the school and escape into Switzerland."

I didn't say anything for a minute or more. The proposition was preposterous. It was full of holes, but I didn't want to scare him off with invective for fear he'd take umbrage and not offer his other proposition.

"What's your other scheme?"

"You'd be dropped in the vicinity of Mannheim as a German soldier and gather intelligence, then escape into eastern France, where we do have some escape and evasion nets."

"Anything else up your sleeve?" I gazed at him intently. "Man, you're trying to serve me a death warrant without a chance of doing anything worthwhile. What documents of any importance would I find in an officers' tactical school? Manuals similar to ours? And if I were able to reach Switzerland, I'd be interned for the duration. The other scheme wouldn't amount to a damn. Whatever order-of-battle information I'd collect would be stale by the time it reached you. I'll consider a calculated risk, but these are shots in the dark."

He looked sheepish. "Guess I didn't balance things out from the operative's point of view. Sorry!"

"In the future, I'd make that number one when deliberating on the feasibility of an operation," was my parting shot as I slammed the door on the way out.

It looked like curtains for me, at least for the near future. Nevertheless, I didn't shut out completely the possibility of a mission since conditions fluctuated daily. Perhaps our rapid advance toward the Rhine would be slowed up, perhaps not. But it was pretty obvious that our lines of communications were being stretched to the limit. Such a situation should trigger a counterattack.

However, this was something I couldn't influence. I'd given notice of my availability and more I couldn't do. Lay off and stop speculating or you'll become a nervous wreck, I chided myself.

Although SO had operations underway in Italy, they didn't require any of us. They had an ample pool of operatives trained for that area. So we just bided our time until SO made up its mind. We were bored and frustrated. Fighting was going on and we weren't in it. We kept making the rounds of the pubs and clubs and roamed around the city.

The Germans introduced a supersonic novelty—the V-2. You could hear the missile only after it hit the target, which was any structure in London. This was eerie. At least with the slower, motor-driven V-I you heard its approach and expected the other shoe to drop. Out walking, you'd get caught short by an air raid alert and have to dash to the nearest air raid shelter. But in spite of all this harassment, the valiant British spirit was quite in evidence. They were good natured and cheerful, yet determined to prevail.

Finally, Special Operations threw in the sponge. Nothing was turning up for the Jeds and SO could no longer justify holding that pool of operatives in Europe. The China theater, including Indochina, was becoming dominant. The decision was made to give the Jeds a thirty-day leave and then on to the Far East with a possible return to Europe for a few of us. We'd be expected to report to our new assignment right after the Christmas–New Year holiday. Before taking off, I repeated my desire to return for an SO mission and was told to keep in contact with OSS headquarters in Washington.

During my leave in southern Florida, I kept in touch with OSS. Toward Christmas, the unexpected enemy counterattack culminated in the Battle of the Bulge. The Allied advance to the Rhine had been delayed. Would that produce a mission for me?

The answer came the day after Christmas. I was reassigned to SO, London. Several days later, I picked up my orders at the somewhat familiar Q Building in Washington but this time as a seeded veteran of OSS.

A few days later, I reached London and reported in at Grosvenor Square.

At the SO branch the same staff was on tap. "Did you spend a good leave? What are the prices like stateside?"

"Costs are up and a bit of rationing is in effect," I informed them. "I've been keeping in shape and brushing up on my German."

"Looks like you might be getting a lot of practice in it. Something is brewing."

After a bit more chitchat with the staff, I was ushered into the SO chief's office.

Gerald Miller, the SO chief, was a former Detroit banker who had been offered an Army commission but preferred to retain a civilian status. He was a friendly, affable person and immediately put me at ease.

"Captain, I understand you've been pestering the staff for a mission in the Reich," he greeted me smilingly.

"I admit I might have been a little pushy, but I'm eager to pull off a job there."

"Well you're in luck, that is if a risky caper can be considered contributing to it," he advised me.

"Mr. Miller, as long as it is an unconventional warfare mission, I'll take it!"

"I had no doubt about that! It's right down your alley."

He then proceeded to give me a condensed version of the mission. "We eventually received intelligence that indicated the final Nazi holdout will be in the redoubt area in the Austrian Alps. The top Nazi leaders are supposed to take refuge there and their SS (black-shirt storm troopers) forces will be the defense element. You will raise a company strength unit of German defectors, military and civilian; conduct subversion, sabotage, and guerrilla actions; and above all capture high-ranking Nazis. You will work out the training and operational aspects and we'll arrange the recruiting details, which you'll utilize. The Paris headquarters will establish your base and training facilities as well as provide a small German-speaking operational staff to assist you. They will also support you logistically. The operation will be conducted in German uniform with appropriate enemy weapons, ammo, and explosives. The mission will be designated Iron Cross and you, as commander, will be under the staff control of Lieutenant Colonel Powell, Paris SO chief. Now, how does all that strike you?"

"I couldn't have asked for anything better. Many thanks for your confidence in my ability."

"Now get together with the staff officer who is writing up the official plan and add whatever details you wish to include. When that's finished, pick up your orders and report to Colonel Powell in Paris."

With that we shook hands and parted as he wished me good luck. I wasn't destined to see him again until 1952 under related but entirely different circumstances.

The major who was developing the plan gave me a copy

to review. It contained all the aspects touched on by Miller but of course in greater detail. I added related factors dealing with a cover story, documentation right down to the German soldier's paybook (Soldbuch), a lengthy list of operational and logistical requirements, and an expanded operational mission.

"Do you know that this will be the largest and most daring European operation to be attempted by SO?" queried the planner.

"But 'Jedburgh' had more personnel and covered a larger area," I reminded him.

"No, this will be the biggest in terms of a solid, unified force that directly will conduct all the action. The Jeds operated in small teams and were widely dispersed, with the resistance performing the combat role. Of all the operations that were planned by SO, this one is tops for size with a direct combat role. Furthermore, it will be the biggest blind drop SO ever attempted. Even the Jed teams were met by reception committees which represented a slice of an ongoing resistance group. You'll be jumping into a void—no local support except what you can generate."

"Major, you're not trying to discourage me?"

"Hell no! Just want to be sure you know all the angles."

"I don't know if you realize it, but you've been making me more eager than ever."

With that, I sped out of that headquarters for the last time with my orders for Paris clutched in my fist.

The Paris OSS headquarters was located on the beautiful Champs Elysées. I loved that boulevard. I hadn't been there since 1938. Although Paris had been occupied by the Germans for more than four years, it was physically still the old Paris. But the gay spirit of the Parisians was subdued, as though they were still in shock. The shops were poorly stocked. Only the best and most expensive restaurants had any variety on their menus and, of course, no tourists were browsing around.

As I walked into the front office, I was welcomed by Capt. Bob Lacoste, a slim, erect soldier who looked you squarely in the eyes and didn't beat about the bush. I immediately took a liking to him. He told me he had arranged quarters for me in the OSS hotel and that he'd get me oriented around town. He indicated they were all excited over my mission. Things had been slow for SO recently and this would be a shot in the arm.

"The old man's waiting for you." Bob showed me in and Lt. Col. Robert (Rip) Powell greeted me warmly.

"Well, we've got lots to talk about. I still haven't received the official mission plan, just a concise memo indicating that we're to set up your training facilities and logistical support. Also, to set up a recruiting team and tap our contacts with German dissidents."

I then briefed Powell on the major details of the UW mission. He appeared impressed.

"I didn't realize it was going to be such a big operation. It's grown considerably since Bob and I dreamt up the initial idea and broached it to London. Took some struggling to sell it and now it's our one big hope. It will keep my staff hopping. Bob will maintain liaison with you on all aspects of the operation. As soon as you've completed the recruiting tour, I'll visit you at your base."

Powell summoned Bob, repeated what he told me, and stressed that everything concerned with the mission would be given top priority.

While Bob was informing me about the recruiting team, a rather stout major came in. "That's Maj. Stuart Pusey," Bob informed me. "He's SI–S4. He'll furnish your logistics support."

I was to see Pusey on his flying trips to my base whenever there was a logistics problem. Bob had set up a four-man recruiting team: Bob, myself, and two other German-speaking officers. Major Pusey had arranged for a civilian car, gas, and funds.

However, there was one important contact we had to make first. Bob told me we'd meet with the head of a German dissident group which had a number of members who had fled to France as refugees. A batch of them had fought with the Resistance and already had been recruited by OSS for behind-the-lines operations. They were in a holding compound in Saint-Germain, just outside of Paris. Bob also advised me that my base would be in that area.

Several days later, Bob and I kept a date with Herr X, whom we christened Karl. We met at a safe apartment whose owner was an absentee American. Since Bob didn't speak fluent German, we conversed in French.

Karl was around sixty, heavily built, and quite secretive. He had lost an arm fighting for the Loyalists in the Spanish civil war. His only pertinent information was lists he had of Germans in French POW camps and additional members of the organization who might be interested in clandestine work. We suspected that the group was commie oriented, but Karl claimed they were just anti-Nazi. However, when Karl claimed that all the individuals he'd obtain for us definitely would fight against the Nazis, that was good enough for us and OSS. It was in line with the philosophy of our OSS chief, General Donovan: "Use them as long as they kill Nazis!"

We arranged for another meeting for the following day so Karl could let us know if he could accompany us on the trip and introduce two of his people whom he thought would be of superior value.

The next day we met at the same location and Karl said he could join us anytime we wished to start. We roughly planned the trip, to a large degree based on the location of the POW camps (enclosures) he had listed. In the meantime, one of Karl's staff would contact the remaining civilian dissidents to whom he had referred.

Then Karl introduced us to his two friends Max and Hermann. What a combination! An assassin and a con man! Max was built like a weight lifter; in fact, he'd been a circus performer. He had a solid jaw, a bull neck, and was a bit ponderous as far as agility went. But it was evident that his tremendous, latent strength made up for it.

I later told Bob, "That Kraut could make a smaller pile of pulp out of you than a python!"

The other chap, Hermann, was quite suave, of medium build, and a persuasive speaker. Both he and Max had fought for the Loyalists (communists) in Spain where they had conducted Intelligence operations. They appeared to be buddies and wanted to work together, particularly in intelligence. I indicated I'd certainly consider their request.

A few days later, attired in OSS-issued civvies, we started out with Karl; Lt. Hans Marchand, Bob's assistant, who would spend a lot of time at my base; and an OSS civilian,

Douglas Bagier. Both Marchand and Bagier spoke fluent German.

After stopping at Cluny and Dijon, we headed for Lyon, the first of our larger POW camp sites.

At Lyon we devised a routine that we repeated at each camp. Bob would present our orders which authorized us to interrogate any POW in the camp. The French War Ministry had affixed its stamp of approval on the orders. A room or a space outdoors would be arranged with a table and chairs. We'd sit around the table with our record books in which we'd make our short evaluations of each man. The guards would produce the men on Karl's list and they'd be interviewed separately. Whenever any of them wanted to be reassured as to their treatment by us and the possibility of early release after their service was ended, our finger man, Karl, would relieve their concern. Of course, the mission was never disclosed. But the POW's definitely were interrogated as to their views on Hitlerism and if they'd fight the Nazis. We also considered their attitude, military background, appearance, and bearing.

From Lyon we went south through the Rhône Valley through Valence and Montélimar. I must admit we had a lot of Côte du Rhône uncorked for us—a delicious vintage. We stopped at Alès where I had my command post in the Maquis days and then to Nîmes where, as a Jed, I'd been dragooned into making a public speech. Next was Marseilles where there was quite a large POW camp, on to Montpellier, then Carcassonne with its medieval battlements and turrets, and finally Toulouse. On the return trip, at Doug Bagier's suggestion, we visited Victor Hugo's château and library where, due to Doug's close friendship with the family, we were entertained and bedded down for the night.

On the route back to Paris, in Limoges, three of our group had severe bellyaches and called for a doctor. He finally concluded that the almonds we had bought at a roadside stand were really horse chestnuts and not edible. I thought at the time that they looked peculiar for almonds and hadn't eaten any. Those who did had subjected their innards to a dose of prussic acid. They'd been conned with a stomachache as a bonus.

Bob and I reviewed all the evaluations and selected more than 125 of the interviewees. We also accepted the German civilians at the holding compound at Saint-Germain. Practically all of the latter had fought with the Resistance. The total ran about 170 men. Bob claimed they'd all be delivered to my base within a week or so and that, according to Major Pusey, my staff would arrive in several days. The household or station complement was already there pitching squad tents, setting up cots, and preparing everything for the arrival of all the personnel.

We drove out to Saint-Germain, about fifteen miles west of Paris, where the base was located. It was a large estate with a typical French manor house, very spacious and comfortable, with many of the original furnishings, but just not grand enough to be in the château category.

After I installed my gear in the master bedroom, which would also serve as my office, we took a tour of the grounds. The estate abutted the forest of Saint-Germain which was also available for training. Actually, I had carte blanche to conduct training throughout the entire countryside. The French police had been advised that a secret training station was located on the estate and that training would be conducted in the general area.

The base appeared to be quite satisfactory except that the local population would soon be aware that something peculiar was going on. However, I was satisfied that, if they didn't know where we'd operate or where our drop zone would be and when we'd jump in, our security was safe enough. Anyhow, whenever I considered security, I always had my tongue in my cheek. How safe were these guys we'd recruited anyway? That was a gamble I had to take.

A lieutenant, a New Yorker from Watertown whose name I've forgotten but whom I shall call Steve Rogers, was in charge of the station complement, all of whom were OSS personnel. Rogers showed me the kitchen, which was well equipped and sufficiently large to feed 180 men; the quarters for Rogers's men and my staff, which were all in the main house; the ammo; and the demolition bunkers and storerooms for weapons and supplies. The GI uniforms and fatigues for the Germans were ready for issue, since that would be their training and service attire. A post exchange would be set up for the convenience of the Americans and the Germans. All our recruits would be paid five dollars a day for their services out of OSS funds.

The Germans would be restricted to their tent quarters. Their mess and dayroom were in tandem squad tents. But the classrooms would be in the salons of the manor house. The mess for the OSS enlisted men and for the officers was also in the main house.

My staff arrived a few days later: Lt. James Lewis (a pseudonym), Staff Sergeant Popovich (a pseudonym), M. Sgt. Theodore Baumgold, and Sgt. John Goldbeck. The latter two were radio operators. All except Lieutenant Lewis spoke German. Lewis spoke French. However, this still allowed him to communicate since the Germans who had been in the resistance movement spoke French. Baumgold was expected, since he'd told me in London when I was trying to cook up a German mission that he'd be interested.

I welcomed the staff and briefed them. "I'm sure you're wondering why you've been assigned to this mission, designated Iron Cross. I'll give you a concise picture of what it's all about. We will conduct our mission somewhere in the Reich, but the area of operations is top secret. So on that score I'll have to leave you in the dark until the appropriate time. The closest I can come and not breach security is that we'll conduct unconventional warfare behind enemy lines—ambushes, raids, destroy lines of communications, commit sabotage, gather intelligence, induce subversion, and generally harass the enemy and capture ranking Nazi leaders. The unit will be composed of a company-size group of German defectors, mostly POW's. We'll operate in German uniforms with enemy weapons, gear, and demolitions and pose as a mountain infantry (Jäger) company. Your job initially is to assist in training the German defectors using your language capability. In addition, you'll keep an eye on them, not as guards but as informants, watching for any signs that would arouse suspicion as to their support of our cause or any conspiracy against our personal safety and security. Remember, what we are and do is always top secret. Here's a copy for each of you of restrictions I've placed on our guests. Any violations will not be tolerated. Any questions?"

"What do we know in regard to their background and loyalty?" asked Lieutenant Lewis.

"Nothing! Except that each has volunteered to fight the Nazis and has been singled out by the leader of a German anti-Nazi resistance organization. It's a calculated risk, not only here but even more so when we're operational in enemy territory. During training, we'll weed out those who can't cut the mustard in terms of ability and motivation. Those who sneak out of here we're well rid of. They won't get far, since we'll report such cases to the French police."

"Then we're really shooting craps," he responded.

"I've balanced that risk against the potential of the mission and have decided to accept that situation. As far as I know, most of our guests are commie inclined or outright communists. Our OSS chief, General Donovan, is satisfied and sticks to his adage, 'If they kill Nazis, we'll use them!' "

"What are our chances if we're captured?"

"Caught behind the lines in German uniform—summarily executed, but preceded by a dose of torture if the Gestapo gets into the act. You'd better remember that when you opted for OSS you were warned that our type of work, behind the lines, is outside the provisions of the Geneva Convention for POW's. If you hadn't accepted that condition you wouldn't be here now."

I allowed that to sink in before continuing. "Now, if any of you are overly concerned about your personal safety, you can drop out now and I'll request a new assignment for you!"

When I added that last stinger, I was satisfied they would not turn down the operation. I guessed right. They looked grim, but they'd stick it out. That discussion had cleared the air as to rationale, determination, and attitude. I thanked them for their confidence and support.

Apparently the staff was behind me and would do their best. Each was well trained, although none except Baumgold had yet participated in a clandestine operation.

Now the trick was going to be to keep the Germans completely engrossed in training; toughen them up; and initially qualify them in individual basic training, since a number of them had not been soldiers—just escapees or refugees from the Nazis. However, some had served with the French Resistance where they did have some training.

I continued my briefing. "Our program will generally include map and compass reading, enemy-weapons training, individual movement, patrol formations, day and night marches with equipment, survival, raids and house clearing, demolitions, sentry elimination, and all aspects of guerrilla warfare and other covert activities. This is a big job and we'll aim to complete it within eight to ten weeks.

"The unit will be organized in platoons for instruction and the same subjects will be taught at the same time, except for the platoon of non-army personnel. Their pace, of course, will be slower. Each of you will be assigned a platoon and will be responsible for its instruction. Since we'll be operating as a German infantry company, whenever feasible, in terms of time to fit it in, we'll participate in German Army close-order drill with the Germans. Each of you will do this as a private and I as a *Gefreiter* (corporal). This will include platoon tactical formations. These drills will be handled by the ranking German in each platoon and a company commander will be selected by me from among the platoon leaders. As soon as the German army equipment arrives, these drills will be performed in German uniforms with German gear and weapons. We'll also use German demolition equipment in our demolition and sabotage training.

"Lieutenant Lewis and I will prepare the detailed training program and scheduling. Until our guests arrive, you sergeants will be detailed to scout out a demolition area, an area suitable for a firing range, damaged or abandoned houses for house-clearing exercises, and a compass run. I will contact the local police to afford assistance in locating these requirements.

"And the last items on this agenda are concerned with our weeding-out process and the unit restrictions as they pertain to the Germans. During training you'll maintain a record on members of your platoons, indicating their attitude, motivation, and soldiering ability. Those who can't meet our standards will be weeded out. Also a Lieutenant Marchand will be attached here to conduct a screening program concerned with weeding out undesirables in terms of ideology, aptitude, rationale, and security in general. As for restrictions, you'll conduct nightly bed checks and the Germans will be strictly confined to their area in our compound when off duty. Orient them well on what's expected: maintenance of quarters, mess, and dayroom areas; policing the tent area; and handling and maintenance of equipment. That's about all for now. Again, are there any questions?"

"None," said Lewis speaking for the staff. "We'll be humping like hell, but it's a wow of a mission!"

I knew they'd feel that way and it encouraged me, because the day would come when our lives would depend on one another.

After leaving the staff, I hunted up Lieutenant Rogers and directed him to ensure we had good, competent cooks and that there would be no skimping—seconds always available. Although we couldn't furnish German beer in our PX, a GI beer ration would be available after training hours.

"Steve, don't think I haven't an ulterior motive in feeding them well, that is provided they put out and don't try to goldbrick. We'll work the ass off them, but they'll be rewarded in this fashion. And after a dose of POW rations, I know that what we'll offer will grab them!"

"I'll let the cooks know the importance you place on their capabilities and I'll see to it that we have a first-class mess," responded Steve, and he headed for the cook's quarters.

The next few days, Jim and I plugged away at the training program. Since I specialized in sabotage, house clearing, raids, and guerrilla tactics, I would handle those subjects as well as familiarizing the platoons with German weapons. I would also handle whatever aspects of covert operations I decided the platoons should receive.

"Jim, I hope this will help out, because you fellows will be busy as hell and I do want our two radio operators to practice their da-de-das daily. When the Germans start arriving, which should be in a few days, form them into platoons and assign our sergeants to them. But be sure to put all the civilian guests into one platoon which you will handle, since a number of them have some understanding of French."

Over the next few days, the Germans were trucked in

from the various POW camps. The first arrivals were those from the OSS holding area close by.

Uniforms and gear were issued and the staff oriented them according to the instructions I had issued. The Germans all appeared quite cheerful and pleased with the arrangements. Lieutenant Rogers advised me that they immediately adjusted to our rations—no waste.

I notified Lieutenant Lewis to assemble them so that I could greet and welcome them. "Have them formed in a U-formation so that they can all hear me and so that I can look 'em in the eye and observe their reactions clearly. Get them lined up right after lunch in front of our headquarters entrance."

As I came out of the entrance, Jim snapped them to attention.

"Put them at ease, Lieutenant."

The men relaxed. From where I stood on the entrance steps, the Germans, dressed in their GI-issue summer uniforms, appeared like any group of GI's. There was an air of expectancy about them. They were going to hear a lot more from me than the cursory exchange that took place initially in the POW camps. They were waiting intently to hear the conditions under which they'd exist or, for some, survive. This was their chance to size me up.

In my ungrammatical but understandable German, I addressed them.

"I am Captain Bank, your commander. I greet you as members of a unit that will work, train, and fight as a team against the Nazis, who have enslaved your country and are destroying it. At the same time, they are daily committing crimes against all of Europe and wherever else they have violated international law. By aiding the cause of the Allies, which is your declared intent, you will share in the Allies' noble struggle and undertaking.

"You will be treated as soldiers, not as prisoners. There are no guards here because I have full faith in each and every one of you. The training will be specialized, rugged, and demanding, but you won't be required to do anything I or my staff won't or can't do. Pay strict attention to your instructors. The better you absorb your training, the more you'll accomplish in the combat phase.

95

"My staff has already oriented and briefed you. You should now be acquainted with the restrictions imposed on you and our general regulations pertaining to your various duties. I want strict obedience to those standing orders and immediate compliance to orders issued by me or any of my staff. Any deviation will not be tolerated. Are there any questions?"

"Ja! Werden wir bezahlt werden?" several called out.

"You will receive five dollars daily. This will be held for you and any purchases you make at the PX here will be defrayed out of that sum."

"Dürfen wir in die Stadt gehen?"

I had expected this one. "No, you can't leave the area to go into town, but I'll see about it later."

I was waiting for the question, "What's our mission and where will we operate." But it didn't pop up, for which I was grateful since I would have had to duck answering it.

"Before I dismiss you, I want to stress again that this won't be a picnic. You will sweat, puff, and wish you were back in a POW camp at times rather than suffer under our grueling schedule. So if any of you want to drop out, do it now. Just raise your hand and you'll be returned to the safe monotony from which we sprang you."

Not a hand appeared.

"I'm sure you'll all make the grade, but if I find any of you unsuitable in any way, you'll be dropped from the program. Lieutenant Lewis, dismiss the formation."

I joined my staff. "Things look promising. I have an idea that most of them will make it. But keep your eyes peeled for flunkers and, at the same time, for platoon leaders. Lieutenant Lewis and I have completed the details on the training schedules and the various subjects we'll teach. They will be posted shortly so you can prepare your lesson plans. We'll be scheduling on a six-day week. I've checked the firing and demolition ranges and the other facilities you've recommended. All are satisfactory. I've arranged with the police to have several flics (cops) in the housing area whenever we conduct house-clearing raids among the bomb-damaged houses.

"Now remember while conducting your instruction to keep your mind on our concept of operations. This will ensure that the subjects you're teaching will be slanted and aimed at developing the unit's proficiency toward accomplishing those goals.

"I'll repeat: As a German infantry company, we'll march in formation openly on the roads to reach objectives, conduct roadblocks, misdirect traffic, and check for Nazi bigwigs. However, when required and the opportunities occur, we'll revert to guerrilla and clandestine activities in order to conduct ambushes, sabotage, subversion, defections, raids, and the kidnapping and seizure of Nazi leaders."

The Germans, formed into four platoons, were ready for training. Those without any former army service were in Lieutenant Ellis's platoon.

When the training commenced, it became quite obvious that Ellis's platoon would progress at a slower pace than the others. This was anticipated, but my concern was whether the Germans were absorbing the instruction. I kept them under close scrutiny and found that Ellis's teaching was being correctly interpreted and the men were learning. The other platoons were breezing through the basic phase; it was duck soup for the veterans.

All the Germans seemed to enjoy the training except for the PT and jogging. For the nonvets, this phase was started without pressure and was gradually toughened. But the vets started up at a fairly rough pace.

"Aber es war nie so schwer in der Wehrmacht!" The vets even complained of the daily four-to-five-mile morning run. But we didn't let up on them. They were to be toughened up fast and those who couldn't take it would be weeded out. From the vets I expected top performance under pressure.

Ellis carefully guided the nonvet platoon through their paces and gradually toughened them up physically. Their basic skills improved. The way they responded to him and to his instruction, given through several interpreters, convinced me that the system would function under operational conditions. In fact, Ellis was picking up a bit of German on the way.

I had set up a routine for myself that permitted me to check each of the platoons daily. Through watching, asking questions, and requesting demonstrations, I could keep my finger on the training pulse. I was satisfied with what I had noted. The training was being absorbed. Later, in the more advanced and in the clandestine and guerrilla phases, the men exhibited even more intense interest and concentration since this was something entirely new to them.

After several weeks, based on the recommendation of the staff, I selected five of the German *Feldwebel* (sergeants) for command assignments: four as platoon leaders and one as company commander. They were combat veterans and appeared to have the desired leadership qualities. I would have to give them special training in their command duties, always reminding them of the fact that my staff members were their seniors.

"I have selected you five sergeants because of your combat experience and the recommendations of my staff. You four will be *Feldwebel* of your platoon and Kurt will be designated as *Oberleutnant* (first lieutenant) and company commander.

"Whenever we conduct close-order drill at this area, you will function in your new capacity, since I and my staff will be in the ranks. Whenever your platoon leader instructs you to assume command of a section of the platoon itself, you will do so and will follow his orders.

"During the operational phase, whenever we are marching in formation, you will be in command, following out my orders at all times. Verstanden?"

"Jawohl, Herr Hauptmann!" (Yes, captain!)

"There will be special instructions in the conduct of your new additional duties whenever it will be convenient to my schedule. Dismissed!"

I would have to fit in the sergeants' leadership and command instruction as it concerned their duties. I was already pinned down several evenings each week training Max and Hermann in intelligence gathering, setting up a network, establishing safe houses, letter drops, and other clandestine-related activities. Max and Hermann would remind me now and then that they had been intelligence operatives, but I wanted to be sure of their performance, since they would be my ears and eyes. They knew their stuff, but I figured there's nothing like being sure. However, when I touched on subversion and creating defections in the German forces, they displayed avid interest. So it looked like Sundays for the command and leadership training, since Sunday would be a rest day for the unit.

Lieutenant Marchand had set up a screening procedure which we hoped would help in eliminating undesirables and possible security threats. But it appeared that it would be a lengthy project.

"How's your head-shrinker program progressing?" I asked him.

"I'm no pro at it, but there's a psychiatrist assigned to assist in getting it on a professional level. However, there are a few men in the outfit about whom I am already doubtful, so some weeding out could start shortly."

"Let's get them out soon if there's a logical basis for it. But I want to review each case first. I don't want to lose any just on speculation. Nevertheless, those who are really doubtful should be out before I start any phase of the clandestine training. Those are secrets with which I don't want them to be walking away."

Bob came by during this early stage and we discussed Marchand's program. I wanted to settle the general concern over security before it might foul up the mission.

"Colonel Powell and I," Bob said, "will spare no effort to develop the best possible screening program. We feel that with the pro taking charge, it will be as effective as it could be under existing circumstances."

As I told Bob, I was afraid that this program under the "pro" could get beyond our local control, up to a higher level, and boomerang. That was what worried me. I was used to taking risks, but only after I had balanced them out. Starting with the major, who wrote the mission in London and stirred the initial ripples of concern over security in his private conversations with me, I had been calculating the risks involved and decided that the value of the mission outweighed them.

Bob agreed that we didn't want to do anything that might abort the mission. "In that case," I concluded, "knowing that accurate screening is impossible with the limited information we have on these people, let's quit fussing and accept the inevitable. Drop the pro idea and let Marchand conduct the simplified screening. But his findings will be revealed only to me and I'll determine who is to be released.

Of course, there will be undesirables uncovered during training who can't meet our standards but who are not necessarily security threats.''

"All right!" he announced. "It's a deal! I'm quite sure Colonel Powell will buy it, because your operation will be the only one we'll have for the Special Operations branch.''

I was glad to note that Bob realized the whole subject was an irritant to me. "Don't get huffy," he continued. "It's your neck and that of your staff, for whom you're responsible. I understand your deep concern that the security aspect might blow up and adversely influence London. Neither of us wants this, so we'll keep Marchand's little program under wraps—just between you, me, and Colonel Powell.''

I was relieved and looked it.

Bob smiled. "Discussion closed! You're a tough, old son of a bitch and that is what's needed most of all!''

The Intelligence training for Max and Hermann was broadened to include the use of minisize German-made cameras. The training was handled by a photography expert sent over from London who also briefed Max and Hermann on the German Gestapo since their cover was posing as Gestapo agents. This included a cover story backed up by proper identification documents forged by our documents section in London. The photography expert also brought several suits, shoes, and other items of clothing, tailored after German models, for which Max and Hermann had been measured.

As the days passed, more and more of the training was concerned with field exercises, which brought the unit to the direct attention of the locals. Mainly, they were intrigued by hearing German used among the troops and instruction and orders being given in that language.

"Comment ça ce fait qu'ils parlent allemand? Qu'est-ce que les Boches font ici?''

I couldn't give them a satisfactory and believable answer. I'd brush off these questions by just saying German was required in the training and the unit was under control of the U.S. Army.

At the end of the day, when we'd be performing close-order drill on the grounds of the estate, passersby would wonderingly say "Qu'est-ce que se passe?" (What is going on?) when they heard "Achtung!" "Vorwärts Marsch!"

"Kolonne rechts!" and other commands barked in guttural tones.

The estate had a high wall shutting it off from the street, but the rest of the property extended to the borders of the forest of Saint-Germain and was open except for a hedge. Our German uniforms, weapons, and gear had arrived— battlefield salvage especially procured for us—and we'd don them for the drill period. At such times I learned from the police that they were flooded with inquiries and reports of imaginary subversive activities. We toned down this practice to a minimum thereafter. But Colonel Powell and his staff got a big charge out of witnessing our formal German drill exhibition in German uniforms which we'd put on for their visits.

The staff and I soon learned the various commands, formations, drill sequences, and manual of arms. Quite different from ours! Except for Bob, who was a frequent visitor, the colonel and his staff had to search in order to spot us hidden in the ranks.

The OSS documents section in London notified Bob to get a personal history statement from me in order to prepare a cover story.

After reviewing it, he grinned. "Why you old bastard, you've lived a life of adventure and you're still reaching for more."

"Well, I'm not exactly looking for the waterhole where, eventually, I'll bump into the tiger."

"Maybe not, but I think you've got a tiger by the tail right now. When instructing these cookies how to use Fairbairn's OSS stiletto on a sentry, don't you kind of wonder whether you'll be the target should they want out once they're in Austria?"

"All right, Bob, you struck a nerve, but I've got confidence in this bunch and no one has taken French leave."

"Aaron, you know them a little better than I do, but let's face it, when the chips are down you might get a lethal surprise."

"Bob, you can say what you like, but I'm determined to see this through. If we get only a few Nazi bigwigs, it's worth the gamble."

Based on my past, the OSS documents section used as a

foundation the fact that I had been a lifeguard and medical gymnast (now called physical therapist) in Nassau, the Bahamas, and Biarritz, France. They reasoned it was the most logical way to rationalize my presence in a German mountain-infantry company. I would certainly be spotted as a foreigner with my ungrammatical German lacking in colloquialisms. I was to be a native of Martinique, because my French, although not deficient in colloquialisms, was somewhat deficient in accent. The OSS figured that the Germans wouldn't recognize what I could claim was a Martinique patois. It was stressed that my enlistment in the *Wehrmacht* mainly was due to the fact that I was a Nazi sympathizer and that I formerly was employed by the German labor office at a German military hospital in Biarritz as a masseur and medical gymnast.

When Bob delivered my documentation, he laid it out for my review. There was a cover story, French *carte d'identité,* and German Army *Soldbuch* (paybook).

"Study your cover so you know it backwards," insisted Bob. "I sure will and from here on I'm Henri Marchand to the unit."

I then requested Bob to have the Air Corps Special Operations (SO) wing that supported OSS select for my approval some drop zones somewhere above the Inn Valley of Austria between Innsbruck and Kufstein. "I'm having a C-47 door-exit mock-up and a parachute-hanging device constructed for preliminary jump training. In the event that I can't get in practice jumps for the outfit, at least they'll know how to exit and handle parachute risers. In that event, it admittedly would be a truncated course and they'd therefore jump without their field packs. Everything but their individual weapons would be in containers."

Bob inferred that preliminary contact had already been made.

I continued detailing my requests. "Remind them that this will not be the usual agent jump. They're to be prepared for a mass drop by platoon echelons of at least two platoons per night depending on the selected drop zone. Should the drop zone appear to be marginal, I would consider jumping in initially with a small pilot team, consisting of me, Max, Hermann, and one of the radio operators and his equipment, to check it out, since it's a blind drop, and guide the plane in."

"I'll take care of all those arrangements," promised Bob.

"While you're at it, one more chore—proper documents and cover for Lieutenant Lewis, who speaks practically no German."

I occasionally checked with the staff on the status of the Germans. The staff had a roster of each platoon for the purpose of evaluation. It was now March 1945, time to start weeding out the least desirable Germans. We came up with a list of about twenty-five which included some names furnished by Lieutenant Marchand. However, none were considered security threats by me, just men who couldn't meet our standards. They were paid and returned to POW status with the request from OSS for early release. The civilians among them were returned to an OSS holding compound. There were some murmurs from their buddies, but when it was pointed out that this procedure was necessary to further ensure the success of the mission, the rumbling stopped.

The remaining men seemed loyal. Only a few ignored my orders to stay on the estate: Sunday bed check would record some absentees, but by now we knew where to find them—the local brothels, either Madame Fifi's or Madame Loulou's establishments. A detail of our personnel would round up the absentees in a couple of jeeps. I discussed this with Max and Hermann, who were the most frequent offenders.

"Haben Sie keine Angst! (Don't worry.) With those good American rations and that wonderful apple pie with ice cream topped with whipped cream, we'll never desert. Take that cook along on the operation and you've got us for good. The only thing we miss is German beer. Unser weltberühmtes Münchner Bräu!"

Even the rich malted shakes from our PX couldn't replace their native brew.

With the early-morning runs, physical training, and cross-country exercises, the men were becoming hard as nails. They had been introduced to our bag of tricks—Fairbairn's OSS mixture of catch-as-catch-can and judo.

One night there was a hell of a commotion. Some members of a Moroccan unit stationed nearby sneaked in to steal whatever they could find in the tent area. Although they were famed as knife fighters, our Germans applied their newly learned rough-and-tumble tactics on them. The Moroccans' North African knives were left behind as those who were able to fled. Except for a few superficial cuts, our men were none the worse for wear. And with those souvenirs and the knives as trophies, the incident ended.

Although some of the Moroccans had to be removed in ambulances to the nearest French Army dispensary, no French military police report was filed since we were a classified unit. But the incident was also proof that at least the French military considered our presence as a favorable nuisance, regardless of the feelings of the local population.

My staff was tickled pink. "These guys can scrap and they don't panic" was the consensus. Max let loose that night! He'd been in the thick of it, with bodies flying in all directions! I was reassured that when the time came the men would fight. As for Max, if I ever needed a bodyguard or an assassination teammate, he'd be it.

While our limited jump training was underway, I never hinted that classroom training might be all they'd get. It wouldn't be the first time OSS personnel had made their initial jump their combat entry. At least they'd have the benefit of a reserve chute, a luxury I hadn't been afforded on my French operational jump.

Around this time, Bob informed me that General Donovan would be coming to Paris shortly on a visit to check on the Special Operations branch. "He wants to see if Special Operations can't get a bigger slice of the operational pie. Special Intelligence is forging ahead with its Intelligence missions and the old man is wondering if we're missing the boat."

During our lengthy stay in London, which we dubbed Operation Lost Motion, we'd heard a lot of anecdotes about the general. I repeated some to Bob. We all thought the world of Donovan and these stories in no way lessened our respect and esteem. In fact, they increased it.

Most of the stories were about his way with the ladies. It seems that there was one waiting for him wherever he went and, since OSS was a global outfit, variety was the name of the game. These liaisons he accomplished without benefit of any particular linguistic ability; a Casanova by any other name. . . . In fact it was bruited about that some of the most attractive OSS girls had vied for his attention.

But there was one of his characteristics that soon was to ring a bell. It seemed that if Donovan considered one of the operatives to be capable, he'd reward him with the riskiest tasks. When the details of Iron Cross were disclosed to the general in glowing terms by Colonel Powell, Donovan wanted to know all about Captain Bank, evidently to assure himself that such a large operation was in capable hands.

Apparently, my chief satisfied him to a significant degree on that score. During the latter part of the briefing, Donovan again referred to Iron Cross.

"Will Bank's commies kill Nazis?" he asked. When reassured, he said that he wanted the mission expanded. "Don't limit it to the capture of Nazi bigwigs. I want Hitler!" And then, banging his fist on the table, "Tell Bank to get Hitler!"

The next day, Bob and the colonel paid me a visit. It was now the middle of April. The colonel inquired as to the readiness status of the unit and I responded that we were combat ready. The only thing lacking was the photos of the drop zone.

"I've got them with me," Bob interjected.

The colonel went out to witness some of the training while I pored over the pictures.

The drop zone (DZ) was above the Inn Valley, in the vicinity of Schwarz, at an altitude of about 4500 feet. It was snow covered. At one end was a canyon and, if you weren't lucky, you could land in it and so could some of the supply canisters. All in all, it was not a DZ I'd ordinarily relish.

"Is this the sole choice available?"

"It's the only one the SO wing selected. It was the most suitable," Bob responded.

"It's a toughie, but I'll chance it. Still, in all fairness to my staff and the unit. I'll tackle it first in a pathfinder jump with my pilot team."

When the colonel returned, he asked for my reaction to the selected DZ and I repeated what I had told Bob.

"Well, here's a tidbit!" offered the colonel. "There's a noncommissioned officers school a mile or more away from the DZ."

After having viewed the photos of the DZ, I felt nothing could shock me. "Colonel, what I told Bob stands."

He laughed. "Even General Donovan heard how persistent you were in London for a mission. We discussed Iron Cross. He indicated that intelligence reports continued to pinpoint your operational area as Hitler's refuge. Based on the persistence of those reports, he directed that your mission be expanded. He's beating the drums for Hitler's head. You'll now march to that cadence. Get Hitler! Preferably alive!"

"Give me a week of training to prepare for this and then set us loose." I almost shouted, this time positively in a state of shock.

That night I lay awake for some time. Wild thoughts—world shattering in scope!—were racing through my mind. The implications of the expanded mission were starting to dawn on me. If we were fortunate enough to carry it off—get Hitler, alive rather than dead—it would be automatically the end of the war. The German General Staff would surrender without doubt. It would be the only time in my recollections of historical events when five guys would be responsible for ending a major war.

And who were those five? Three sergeants, one lieutenant, and one captain. What a field day the press would have! What a story! World attention would be focused directly on us.

Then I fell asleep before my thoughts could magnify further. Unfortunately, for security reasons, I could not impart this vital piece of information to my staff. But I did tell them that we wouldn't be hanging around much longer and that did spark them. They were ready to sustain the hot pace I set for what I hoped would be the final week of training.

Again the raiding and house-clearing course I had taken outside London proved its worth. It had already done so in the streets of some of the French towns during Maquisard days. We had conducted raids of residences, apartment houses, and office buildings in partially bombed-out areas that we'd been using, but not as intensively as now.

The colonel and Bob came to witness some of the last-minute activity. I could see they were impressed. A midget couldn't have crawled out and evaded our interior and exterior zones of fire, and reserve guard details would have run into a buzz saw in trying to relieve a besieged headquarters or hideout. Silent kidnapping from various types of houses was practiced as well as roadblocks and selective ambushes.

One of the exercises the colonel and Bob witnessed was a raid on a building right in Saint-Germain by one of the platoons under the command of its German platoon leader. None of the U.S. staff was involved according to Bob, who could recognize them. However, the enemy detail of sentries and relief guard was made up of some of our station complement.

The raid was to take place toward dinner time, in daylight, and therefore the approach had to be clandestine—without uniforms or exposed weapons—in order not to alert the enemy. The target building was located on a square into which three or four streets emptied. There was a café on the corner where a number of people at outdoor tables were having predinner Pernod or other apéritifs. Some individuals had baskets of flowers or groceries or netted bags with baguettes (long loaves of French bread) on their tables or resting on the pavement.

The colonel, leaning against a wall, was getting fidgety. "I don't see any of your crew except the enemy detail. When is the action to take place?"

"Oh, in about five minutes," I answered.

A number of pedestrians were passing us all the time carrying bundles, evidently with goodies for the dinner table.

The colonel looked at his watch several times, then straightened up in anticipation. "It's H hour!"

At that moment, a number of the café crowd rose, picked up their baskets and bags, and started to walk toward the target. Then, in response to a low whistle, they yanked Schmeissers from among the flowers and baguettes, dropped the baskets and bags, and dashed for the target. A number of the passing pedestrians did likewise, their goodies now transformed into submachine guns.

A group of buxom ladies sauntering by near the two sentries suddenly raced to assault them. As their attack went home—their swirling skirts exposing bulky, hairy legs, and millinery and flying wigs baring tough, whiskered faces and bull necks—it became apparent they were no ladies!

What looked like a mob stormed the target building and broke into three distinct teams. The interior assault team burst into the building, the exterior security element took up its positions, and the unit to pin down the relief guard headed for its location.

It all happened faster than the telling. Gazing at the scene, especially the rubbish of baguettes and table goodies in the gutter, the colonel could only utter, "I'll be damned!"

Bob, after controlling his laughter, added, "What a masquerade! And by the brutes attending your 'Dingdong Boarding School for Mayhem'!"

"Maybe I ought to substitute dramatic arts for mayhem," I suggested with a grin.

Training for Iron Cross continued. We slaved day and night; there was no letup. I drove the platoons to the limit. Everyone sensed that we were finally rushing to a climax. All the German equipment was inspected and we spent a final day on the range, firing all our German weapons— Mauser rifles, Schmeisser submachine guns, Luger pistols, and even the antitank Panzerfaust.

I was marching to Donovan's cadence but at double time. We had to be ready and we had to be able to operate with precision and perfection. We'd only get one chance—the chance of a lifetime.

The final stint was a meeting of my staff and the Germans whom I had selected as company commander and platoon leaders. I charged the German leaders with the operational control of their commands.

"Sie konnen auf uns zählen, Herr Hauptmann" (You can count on us, captain) was their response.

"Vergessen Sie nicht mich Gefreiter Marchand zu nennen!" I reminded them. I wanted them to call me Corporal Marchand because my *Soldbuch* (paybook) indicated that rank and so did the insignia on my German uniform.

I explained that Goldbeck and Baumgold would be almost totally occupied with cipher and codes and operating and maintaining the radio, and that the lieutenant and sergeant would assist me in planning and general supervision. I was satisfied that everyone knew the responsibilities and duties of the command echelon. To clarify Max's and Hermann's status, I added that I'd retain them for special tasks.

I'd been sending signals to Bob through his staff assistant to alert the packing station at the OSS staging area that our equipment would be arriving shortly and to arrange for its transportation from my base. The lieutenant advised me that they were handling this and not to be concerned. I guess without realizing it I'd been putting poor Bob and the SO staff under extensive pressure. But after all, it was our necks that were at stake. At least the preliminaries had to come off OK.

When a bit over a week had passed, Bob showed up. "The colonel wants you to come back to Paris with me, prepared for a trip of up to three days. He's arranged to pay a visit to Seventh Army G-2 (Intelligence) so you can be briefed on the Intelligence in which they'd be interested."

As we drove back to Paris, I grumbled about the loss of time involved. But Bob stated that Seventh Army Command had been informed by OSS London that there'd be a large, covert operation in the redoubt area and, since it was the area toward which they were advancing, this coordination effort was necessary. That sufficed to shut me up.

Upon arriving at the Seventh Army Command in Germany, we had a conference with the G-2 and G-3 (operations). I gave a concise briefing on my mission and the G-2, Colonel Quinn, informed me of the Essential Elements of Information (EEI) in which he was interested. No doubt it was necessary, but with me straining at the leash, it seemed very time consuming. I tried to restrain that free-wheeling attitude, but it was difficult.

However, there was one item that concerned me—a recognition signal if Seventh Army troops crashed into the redoubt area. This would be awkward since we'd be in enemy uniforms. It was suggested that, at the sight of a U.S. unit, my closest man would raise his right arm and give the code word Iron Cross in English. We agreed on this, although we all realized that shouting "enemy in sight" would usually draw fire from U.S. troops. I hoped that it would work.

During that quick trip, the colonel often noted that apparently all the German farm labor was conducted by women. He kept repeating, "They must be scraping the bottom of the barrel for manpower."

Whenever we stopped to munch on our C rations on the side of the road, the farm women would collect near us and ask for some.

"Hell, they've got plenty to eat on the farms. It's the urban people who are hungry," the colonel would remark. "Tell them to bug off! No fraternization allowed."

The women would leave and then he'd say that he hated to have to act nastily toward peasant women. "I bet they are not cheering for the Nazis now."

I agreed. I felt no hatred toward the women, but of course their men hadn't invaded our country.

When we got back to Paris, Bob alerted me to be prepared to leave with my pilot team within a few days of his call. Sergeant Baumgold had a badly sprained ankle and therefore Goldbeck replaced him as radio operator. Goldbeck and I would jump in U.S. uniforms, Max and Hermann in their German-cut civvies. They had been issued their Gestapo identity papers and ration books since they'd pose as Gestapo agents.

The German uniforms for the radio operator and me, plus Schmeissers and ammo, were stashed in bundles, as were extra clothes for the two Germans and accessories for all of us. The suitcase radio and the hand generator were packed separately. Luger pistols in shoulder holsters were toted by Max and Hermann. Goldbeck and I carried .45's holstered to our pistol belts. The unit was just told that we were going on a special exercise. Once we were in, Bob would issue deployment orders to Lieutenant Lewis on my request from the field.

Bob called and we left in a command car with a three-quarter-ton truck following with all the gear. We met at the safe apartment where Bob gave me a money belt with gold coins, since German marks were almost worthless due to an insane level of inflation. Bob also gave me a gold ring of such thickness that, when worn on my ring finger, the adjoining fingers, particularly the pinkie, were pushed away from my ring finger at quite an angle. The ring was to be used to bribe my freedom if I was captured. But I didn't put much faith in that, although it was nice having it.

We then drove to Dijon and were installed in the OSS staging compound or the Joe-house—the second time I'd been quarantined in one. Our gear was dropped off at the packing shed located close to an 8th Air Corps field that, in addition to regular operations, handled OSS agent flights. We were full of beans, anxious after all our preparations to become operational.

There were other Joes (agents) waiting to be infiltrated at the château, but we didn't mix with them. They had several officers keeping them under wraps just as Bob shepherded us. But you'd see them at mealtime or walking around the grounds and you'd wonder where they were going to drop and with what intelligence mission they were charged, since we knew they were all SI types.

The following day, Bob took me along to the 8th Air Corps operations to check on our flight.

"Things look bad. The Alps are bogged in, so you're scratched for tonight," we were notified.

I was downcast and Bob tried to cheer me up. "Come on! We'll go back to the château and brush this off with a good run and workout."

But it didn't help much. I told Bob, "We've got to get in and soon, because Seventh Army is on the move. Let's notify air ops that I'll risk a daylight jump if it's easier in terms of weather to get in."

"It's your neck, Aaron, but I'll go along with your suggestion."

The next day, we received the same devastating news. When Bob told them I was agreeable to a daylight jump, air ops said that they'd consider it.

We puttered the day away, took Max and Hermann and the radio operator for a walk and pep talk, and had a few predinner drinks at the château bar, which cheered us a bit.

The weather over the Austrian Alps continued to be bad. Bob told air ops that my team would jump out of any type of plane that had a chance of getting through, but it didn't help. It seemed the weather was determined to keep us out.

A few days later, Seventh Army cracked into the Inn Valley and Bob got a call from OSS London that the mission was scratched.

Years later, I heard that OSS rather than the weather had

been the main contributor to aborting the mission. OSS had decided—evidently under pressure from the State Department—that it wouldn't be a good policy, with the war winding down, to drop more than a hundred suspected commies into Austria. Also, since there was considerable danger, particularly for the U.S. personnel involved, it was determined that the risk was no longer acceptable.

# CHAPTER 6

# Over the Hump: China

We headed back to Saint-Germain heavyhearted, with the steam taken right out of us, our tails between our legs. En route, Bob and I discussed the lousy turn of events. I told him that I was pissed off completely and that I was considering reassignment to China. "Bob, I'll contact you on that score tomorrow. I think Baumgold still wants some action."

"Let me know. Maybe you'll shake the abort jinx in China."

I checked with Baumgold and called Bob the next day to pass on my request for reassignment to OSS China for both of us. Bob called back an hour or so later and said that Colonel Powell had approved the reassignment and, as a bonus, added two weeks of R and R.

Within a couple of weeks, my staff, except for Sergeant Baumgold, was reassigned. The Germans were shipped back to a POW camp with the promise that OSS would obtain their early release. The civilians were released by OSS to remain in France if they wished. Baumgold, who would accompany me to OSS China, and I started two weeks of R and R.

I stayed in the former holding compound in Saint-Germain and enjoyed a lot of recreation by entertaining Bob; the SO staff; my former station complement commander, Lt. Steve Rogers; and of all people Michel, my French operation liaison officer and bodyguard, and his charming wife. By devious means, Michel had learned the location of OSS Paris and had left his calling card there for me, should I show up.

We had a ball. Steve took care of the rations and booze and we hired a French chef. But I wasn't rehabilitated. I still rankled over the aborted mission.

It was during the hiatus in duty status that Bob reminded me to turn in my gold ring and coins to Major Pusey.

When I complied, I handed him my golden hoard, saying, "I don't want any souvenirs of that debacle," but not with any conviction as I longingly watched them disappear into a thick manila envelope.

When the R and R was over in June 1945, Baumgold and I were flown from Paris to Kunming, China, by way of Cairo, where I managed to visit the Pyramids and sample a drink at the old Shepherd's Hotel. We next touched down at Din Jan in Assam, India, the tea-growing center. At a tiny OSS compound, while awaiting final clearance to be flown over the Himalayas to China, I met some of the English plantation managers.

They were somewhat bored by their dull existence and welcomed new faces. I was overwhelmed with invitations and passed some pleasant evenings in their company. They adhered religiously to the British overseas custom of dressing for dinner and not drinking before sunset. Had it not been for them, the layover would have been a boring interlude for me.

We then flew over the "hump" to Kunming. On landing, when the door of the plane opened, a horrible odor assailed me.

"What's that?" I questioned.

The crew told me, "That's China! But you get used to it."

The odor was human manure (night soil). After a few days, I didn't notice it any more.

Evidently Colonel Powell had sent a favorable report, to say the least, to Special Operations China because after only a few days I was given another hot mission. I was to arm, train, and command a company of Indochinese soldiers of the French Army and three French officers, all of whom had escaped from northern Indochina (Tonkin) after the Japanese invasion. The mission was to infiltrate on foot into that area; raid a certain Japanese divisional headquarters along the Red River, which flowed from China southeast through Hanoi and Haiphong; and disrupt communications and hit targets of opportunity along the river and the railroad that paralleled it.

From the Chinese border, the distance to the area was approximately 130 miles through rough and mountainous country which was under Japanese control. This in itself was quite a challenge. The only Intelligence available was a presumed location for the Japanese divisional headquarters. In order to infiltrate with any success, much of the route would have to be by map and compass, since for security reasons we couldn't travel openly in the Red River Valley or on the roads.

Sergeant Baumgold would be the lone radio operator and a Lieutenant Irving was assigned to me. Irving had not yet been in action or on any mission. He was SO trained and raring to go. The three French officers, one captain and two lieutenants, were career officers, but had never undergone any guerrilla training. The troops, except for some of the noncoms, spoke hardly any French and Irving's was quite basic.

I ran the French officers through a truncated, concise course in guerrilla tactics, basic demolition, and sabotage. Then we repeated the training for the troops using the officers as interpreters. The troops appeared to absorb the tactical training. Only the noncoms were exposed to the handling and use of demolitions and the basics of sabotage. Carbines were issued and basic weapons training followed. When the men were proficient in assembling, disassembling, loading, and cleaning the weapons, we marched them to the range for familiarization firing. For regular troops, the result was disastrous. They couldn't hit the side of a barn.

"Comment tirent-ils le fusil?" I asked.

The captain responded that the men were fair with the rifle, but that this was a new weapon for them.

This was a sorry excuse, since at one hundred yards any rifleman can do just as well with a carbine. The officers and

I had noted that most of the troops didn't know how to sight (aim). So we put them through the basics of aiming and firing until they started to hit just the outer circles on a bull's-eye target. Time didn't permit making marksmen out of them!

In the meantime, I had Irving working on an equipment list. Each man would carry a basic load of ammo, dried fish, cooked rice, a blanket, and a change of socks and underwear. We would have C rations, rice, demolitions, grenades, extra ammo, and medical supplies airdropped as we progressed. We'd shoot or trap our fresh meat—wild pig and deer.

Because of the dismal general status of the unit in ordinary infantry training, we were falling behind in terms of the time schedule I had established. But by early July, I figured we had accomplished all we were going to. The outfit was as ready as it would ever be. The French officers concurred and admitted that, during the time the troops had been in China, they'd all had little training.

I notified the SO staff that we were ready to be trucked south to within about twenty miles of the Indochinese border, where we'd start our march, and requested the issuance of our marching equipment and supplies.

I was then advised that SI had just gotten some pertinent intelligence concerning my mission and that it was being analyzed. Based on the results, a takeoff date would be determined.

Warning signals started to sound in my mind. "Damn it! Had my abort jinx followed me all the way to China?"

I didn't have to wait long. The next day I got the news! "The mission is scratched," the SO chief advised me.

"Why?"

"SI reports that if we infiltrate any French personnel or indigenous French army elements, the local guerrillas of Ho Chi Minh's Viet Minh will turn from harassing the Japanese to attacking them. They will not countenance the return of French elements."

This was a blow, although I was intuitively expecting something on that order. To have this happen to me twice in succession at the last moment numbed me. I told the chief, "I still want a mission in Indochina, regardless."

He nodded. "We'll keep in touch."

I hung around waiting. The Operational Groups were encamped a few miles out of Kunming. So I looked up Lt. Col. Al Cox, their chief, as well as a number of other CG's I'd known stateside. They cheered me up a bit. They were training selected Chinese Nationalist army personnel in guerrilla warfare and also operated a jump school for them.

The jump course was conducted in a valley, which for some reason had uplifting warm wind streams flowing down from the hills above. Since most of the Chinese were small and light in weight, a number of them when parachuting would get caught in one of those fluke uplifting winds and would suddenly go heavenward, resisting the normal gravitational pull.

A number of the ex-Jeds were in the field on operations in China and a few, like Shirley Trumps, had conducted some long-range reconnaissance patrols in northern Tonkin (Indochina). Jack Singlaub was also on tap for a POW rescue mission on one of the offshore islands. During the Vietnam period, he commanded SOG, which performed clandestine and covert operations in South Vietnam. Herb Brucker, although not a Jed, had operated periodically in France for SO and had just returned from the Chinese boondocks, where everyone called him Frenchy, since he was Alsatian by birth. I rubbed shoulders with Brucker only for a short time, but we were to become closely associated from 1952 on.

Right after the first atom bomb was dropped on Japan, I was assigned to a politically oriented team that was flown to Hanoi. Captain Patti was the team leader and I was charged with investigating Japanese war crimes and apprehending those responsible for them. In the investigative sphere, I made some progress. The Japanese Kempei Tai (Secret Intelligence) agents had on numerous occasions tortured downed American pilots as well as natives who had been aiding and hiding them. During this time, Patti arranged a release schedule with the Japanese to free in increments the French officers who were imprisoned by them. The officers' families were living unmolested in the Métropole Hotel in the center of Hanoi. However, their fear of the Japanese was now transferred to the Viet Minh, who

117

had assumed a very threatening attitude. Our presence at the hotel, where we were quartered, allayed their fears to some extent.

Shortly thereafter the mission was scratched. Patti and one other officer remained as observers of Ho Chi Minh and his Viet Minh staff who were in the throes of forming an independent government and nation.

# CHAPTER 7

# Indochina: Kicking the Abort Jinx

While marking time, a promotion list, loaded with Operational Groups and ex-Jeds, was posted. I didn't have to read far down the roster to find I was now a major—a bit of consolation for my hard luck with aborted missions! Perhaps my luck would change!

Again I went through a waiting period. Toward the latter part of August, I was given a mission to search for hidden POW camps and French refugees in the Vientiane area of Laos and south to the 16th parallel. The secondary effort was to report on general conditions in the area. The team of which I was the leader consisted of nine officers and enlisted men and was a mixture of SO and SI personnel. My executive was Maj. Charles (Mike) Holland.

Mike had suddenly shown up when I was in Hanoi. It appears that he had been infiltrated north of Hanoi to help train Ho's guerrillas, but had been picked up by the Japanese. They, in turn, handed him over to the Viet Minh after the atom bomb was dropped. While the Japanese were escorting him to Hanoi, Mike met Ho, who apparently took a liking to him.

Mike was a husky devil who'd been a college football player. He was tough, quite a comedian, and partial to the fair sex and hard liquor. We served together in the 187th Airborne Regimental Combat team during the Korean War.

By this time, Baumgold had been shipped stateside and I had a new radio operator. One medic was included in the team. The intelligence officer was Lt. Alger Ellis, who would report on personalities in the political, military, and economic fields.

Since the prime mission was to obtain and facilitate the release of Allied POW's, either by diplomacy, guile, or direct action, a large store of medical supplies was issued as well as food—powdered eggs, dry milk, bouillon, oatmeal, rice, dehydrated vegetables, and canned food. All this was packed into containers and bundles. The radio, weapons, and ammo were in several specially marked containers.

Early in September, we loaded up on a C-47. On the team was a Thai interpreter, who, it was later ascertained, was an agent of the Chinese Nationalist Tai Li (Intelligence Service).

After flying for some time, the pilot called me into the cockpit and stated that he couldn't find the drop zone, which was the Vientiane airfield, and that he didn't have too much fuel left to search around. That confounded abort jinx was still following and clinging to me and this would be the last crack at a mission I'd have in this war. I studied the map and the terrain, showed the pilot what direction to take, and kept my fingers crossed. I figured that he'd flown too far south and east. I growled to myself, I'll lick you yet, you goddamn jinx!

The pilot changed course. As time passed, I became more and more concerned.

Suddenly the jump master yelled, "Red light! Hook up!"

By luck, fate, or my sense of direction, I'd finally buried that damn jinx. We were over the Mekong River approaching Vientiane. I was leading the jump stick. We were hooked up and, when the green light appeared, I was out the door as the jump master shouted, "Go!"

The jump was almost uneventful personnelwise, although the drop zone was alongside the Mekong River and we could have had a good dunking. But a number of bundles landed in swampy areas. While the plane was making its equipment drop, I noted that our medic was still on the ground and holding his ankle. He was evidently suffering from pain and shock from either a badly sprained or cracked ankle. We

**Colonel Aaron Bank, Commander 10th Special Forces Group, 1952**

**Author practicing instinctive firing.**

**Lieutenant Herbert Brucker on left, with Captain Leon de Meis, USA, as members of OSS team Ibex. Haian, Northern China, 1945.**

23.11.1902:.......born in ST.PIERRE,Martinique,

Religion,Status:..Catholic, single.

15.3.1880:........Father: dies in 1920 of Myocarditis.
                  He was an accountant in the Rum Factory St.
                  James,Society An== Coloniale, rue Ernest
                  Deproge 26, Fort de France.

12.2.1882:........Mother: Marie nee BONEL (BONEAU) born in -MARSEILLES.
                  She is still living in MARTINIQUE.
                  I have not seen her since 1941.

1907:.............When I was 5 years old, we moved from ST.PIERRE
                  to FORT DE FRANCE.

                  Home Address:  Rue Victor Hugo, 62.

                  Population: Fort de France 46,000,
                          "    St.Pierre     4,300.

                  Education:

1908-1918:.......Lycée Schoelcher until 1918,

1918-1919:.......Ecole Commerciale.

                  Originally it was my parents and my own wish to
                  become an accountant like my father but, during
                  my study at Ecole Commerciale I developed an
                  aversion against this profession.  On the other
                  hand, during all my youth I was interested in
                  sports and medicine.  Because of my father's
                  early death it was financially impossible for me
                  to study medicine, so I decided to try to make
                  a living as a Masseur and Gymnastic Teacher in the
                  rather fashionable Spas around Fort de France.
                  (Les eaux d'Absalon, de Didier et de Moutte).
                  After a while I succeeded in having many fashion-
                  able people as my clients, besides I was employed
                  on a part-time basis at the Clinique Pasteur as a
                  Therapeutic Masseur.

                  After the German occupation of France economic
                  conditions on the island deteriorated, I lost
                  quite a few of my well-to-do clients; therefore I
                  could not earn enough money, especially as I had
                  to support my mother too.  On the other hand,
                  I knew that for a trained masseur like myself,
                  there would be plenty of work in France,where the

                  Germans maintained many hospitals. So I
                  sailed on the steamer'Mont Viso'
                  (500 GT) - (Soc.Gen de transports
                  Maritimes a vapeur, S.A.) from Fort de
                  France to Marseille via Casablanca.
                      Left Fort de France 11.11.41,
                      arrived Casablanca    7.12.41,
                      left Casablanca       1.1. 42,
                      arrived Marseille    13.1. 42.

                  After my arrival I enquired at the German
                  Labour Office and was told to come back
                  in 2days.  I did so and got a slip and was
                  told to report to the Res.Lazarett at
                  Biarritz, there I worked for about two years

                  The population considered me a collaborator
                  and my feelings and my experiences actually
                  were and made me pro-german.  When my
                  superiors told me that they will see to it
                  that I get a good job and will improve my
                  position if I would join the German Army,
                  I decided to do so.

                  Although jobs in the same capacity did not
                  materialize, I never regret this step.

                  I possess the following papers:-

                  1) French Identity Card,
                  2) Soldbuch Ersatz.

**Brigadier General Russell Volckmann.**

**Key members of Field Training Committee. L to R: Captain Dorsey Anderson, Major Jack Striegel.**

```
                HQ & HQ DETACHMENT              • S E C R E T •
            OFFICE OF STRATEGIC SERVICES        •Auth; CO, Hq & Hq Det.•
          EUROPEAN THEATER OF OPERATIONS        •     OSS, ETOUSA.      •
                UNITED STATES ARMY              •Initials; [signature]  •
                    (FORWARD)                   •Date; 30 April 1945    •
                                                .......................
```

                                                APO 887
                                                30 April 1945

300.4-AMS

SUBJECT:  Orders.

TO      :  Captain AARON BANK, 01314241, Inf.
           Sgt. John B. Goldbeck, 32907131


        1.  You WP o/a 30 Apr 45, from this Hq. to a secret destination for the
purpose of carrying out a secret mission and upon completion of this mission,
you will return to your proper station.

        2.  Travel by military, naval or commercial aircraft, belligerent
vessel, rail and/or motor transportation is authorized.

        3.  TCMT. TDN. 60-136 P 433-02 A 212/50425, Auth; Ltr, Hq European T of
Opns, Sub; Auth to Issue T/O's, dtd 22 Nov 44, file AG 300.4-MPM.

        4.  Personnel named above will be carried on all records of this Head-
quarters as "present for duty".

                    By order of Colonel FORGAN:

                                            STANLEY M. HOLBERG,
                                            1st Lt., QMC.
                                            Ass't. Adjutant.

DISTRIBUTION:

Ea pers. concerned--3
SO Branch----------1
Central Records-----2

**Capt. Carl Bergstrom. Adjutant and S1.**

**Maj. Ray Doucett.**

**Lt. Col. George Gormlie S2 (later Group Executive Officer).**

**Major Art Suchier S3.**

**Bill Druex.**

A 10th Group jump. Author in center.

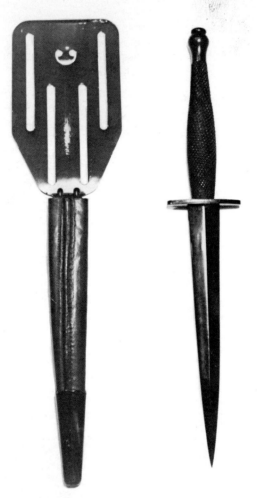

OSS stiletto and sheath—a direct copy of the British Fairbairn-Sykes fighting knife. Only 5000 of these knives were made. Photo courtesy of Robert Buerlein, President of the American Historical Foundation.

signaled the plane to land and the medic was evacuated. We'd have to do without one.

A crowd of Laotians had appeared and they helped us gather and retrieve the containers and bundles. I managed to requisition from a local garage a truck onto which we loaded the bundles and canisters. One of the mechanics offered to drive for us.

Our first find was fourteen French refugees in the Vientiane hospital. They didn't wish to be evacuated, so we supplied them with scarce food items and medicines. We stayed in the area for a few days combing it for POW camps, with negative results. Local Laotian officials were interrogated, but they had no knowledge of such camps anywhere in that part of Laos.

Since there was no passable road south from Vientiane in Laos, we ferried across the river to Siam and headed southeasterly on a reasonably good road. Just a short distance from Vientiane and on a bend of the Mekong, we reached Nong Khai, where we were informed that the nearest large Japanese troop concentration was Savannakhet and that they were no longer functioning as occupation troops. They were waiting for the order to move into Siam, where they were to surrender to the British.

En route, we crossed the Mekong to the Laotian side wherever there was a sizable village, and checked with the natives. They all confirmed that no Japanese troops or POW camps were in the locality.

At several points on the Siamese side of the Mekong, we noted what apparently were British SAS personnel, unpacking weapons from containers. I wondered for what they were destined and for whom.

We finally reached Nakhon Phanom, Siam's provincial capital. I met the governor, a stout, jolly Siamese, who turned out to be very cooperative and helpful. He and his staff spoke fluent English. I explained that we were only passing through, since Siam was not our theater of operations. It was in the Southeast Asia Command under Lord Mountbatten. Nevertheless, the governor invited us to stay with him anytime. He offered us the use of his launch whenever we wished to ferry back and forth on the Mekong.

Thakhet was the Laotian town on the opposite shore. Our driver advised me that it had a passable road running south to Savannakhet and one leading east to the Vietnamese coast road.

I conducted a reconnaissance of Thakhet and met the local officials, who offered us the former French governor's house, the best one in town. It was located along the river at the ferry landing. The officials also confirmed that no Japanese troops were in the Laos north of Savannakhet.

We released the driver and truck and moved all our supplies and equipment to Thakhet and settled into the governor's house.

The first order of business was on the northern fringe of the town, investigating the condition of around eighty French refugees whom we had discovered on our original reconnaissance. The refugees were in need of certain foods and medicines, which we amply supplied. They had been interned at their present location by the Japanese. But with the outbreak of hostilities by the French commandos, they were concerned about how the Laotians would treat them. I offered to evacuate them to the Siamese side of the river, which was under Southeast Asia Command. They said they'd wait and see, evidently hopeful that the French shortly would be in control again.

The team searched the area, but without any positive results. By this time, we had met most of the town fathers as well as one member of the Laotian royal family, Thao Pheng. He obtained a vehicle for our use and a driver.

The day we moved into Thakhet, I witnessed the burial of at least a dozen people, half of whom were women. The dead were lying in crude caskets and, before the covering boards were nailed on, I was shown their wounds. The Laotian conducting the ceremony especially pointed out a number of wounds, even on some of the women, that looked like punctures that had been made with bayonets. I asked the Laotian what had been the cause of all those casualties.

He referred me to Thao Pheng, who invited me to his residence where he said he'd explain.

Thao Pheng was quite cultured and in his flawless French

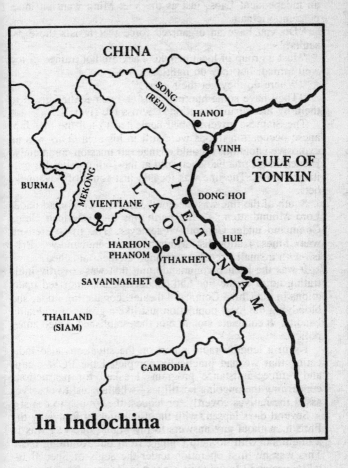

CHINA

SONG (RED)

HANOI

VINH

GULF OF TONKIN

BURMA

MEKONG

VIENTIANE

DONG HOI

L A O S

HUE

HARHON
PHANOM

THAKHET

V I E T N A M

SAVANNAKHET

THAILAND
(SIAM)

CAMBODIA

In Indochina

said, "Ce sont les français. They infiltrate from the south almost every night and attack the town, trying to take control. We don't need or want them back. We wish to have an independent Laos, just as the Viet Minh want an independent Vietnam."

"Do you have an organized force that resists these assaults?"

"Just a group of local people. They are not trained or too well armed, but they do fight back."

"Where do they get their arms?"

"They have some hunting guns and some rifles given to them by the Japanese stationed across the river."

The Siamese governor had neglected to tell me that Japanese occupation troops were still in his area. This was an explosive situation. It could change our mission completely. French Indochina had been split at the 16th parallel for military control. The line was located just south of Savannakhet.

South of the line was the Southeast Asia Command under Lord Mountbatten. To the north was the American China Command under General Wedemeyer. The troop element was Chinese Nationalist. Mountbatten's command was British with a small French commando element attached.

It was the French commando unit that was covertly infiltrating north of the line and conducting unauthorized operations in the China Command theater, conducting raids, and bloodying the local population just like a group of goddamn bandits, in complete violation of the established Allied zonal policy.

I sent a lengthy radio report on the situation, also indicating that we had practically completed the POW-camp- and refugee-assistance program. I asked for instructions concerning the ongoing hostilities—whether just to observe, assist the natives covertly, or request the French to desist.

Several days lapsed, with the usual nightly forays by the French, without any answers to my urgent query. I was in a dilemma, with no help coming from our Kunming base. This was my first operation under the aegis of Special Intelligence and I found their support inadequate now that they were faced with a Special Operations problem—the arming and training of natives. Or were they just too craven to take a position? Their responses glaringly avoided addressing the problem.

I discussed the situation with Mike and Lieutenant Ellis. We had just completed checking further south in the Savannakhet region, also without any positive results.

"Mike, we're just sitting here on our asses while the French are stomping around our backyard like a bunch of bandits, committing wholesale murder without the knowledge and certainly without the authority of the China Command."

"What are we going to do about it?" asked Mike.

"You and I are going to take a quick jaunt to Savannakhet and requisition sufficient gas from the Japanese garrison to sustain a blitz trip to China Command, Hanoi headquarters. Perhaps they'll give us some guidelines after being advised of these violations."

I first contacted Thao Pheng. I asked him if the Japanese were still slipping him arms and ammo. He said they were, mostly now from Savannakhet, and that a few mortars had also been received.

With the local force commander, who had served as a native soldier in the French army in Indochina, Mike and I went and reconnoitered the infiltration routes used by the French in their nightly approach to the town. I suggested to the local force commander there some likely ambush areas and told him that this would be a good way to discourage the French from any further assaults. While we were in the area, I noticed a Japanese officer instructing some of the locals in the use of the mortar and grenades, but I made no comment.

Thao Pheng told me they would follow my hints and instruct their units in the ambush techniques I'd explained to them. I asked him to let us know the results.

When Mike and I arrived in Savannakhet, we made contact with the colonel of the Japanese regiment garrisoned there. He understood sufficient French for me to communicate with him. He invited us to have lunch with him and his staff. During the meal, I laid my demand on him for the equivalent of four or five fifty-gallon drums of gasoline. He complied, ordering one of his staff to have a truck, loaded with the required gas drums, follow us when we left.

Meanwhile, Mike had been glancing with an appreciative but possessive eye at the colonel's samurai sword.

The colonel had noticed. "I can see your major is extremely interested in my sword, but he has been considerate enough not to ask for it."

"Yes, I believe he'd like to have it," I responded.

"He looks like an athlete. Is he perhaps a wrestler?" asked the colonel.

"Yes, he played football and wrestled on his college team."

This seemed to please him. "Would your major be willing to wrestle one of my lieutenants to try and win the sword? Would you permit it?"

"But Mike wrestles catch-as-catch-can, American style."

"No matter. My man will use Japanese style and yours American."

I explained to Mike what the colonel had in mind.

"I'll wrestle any day for a samurai sword," said Mike with a flamboyant air.

"You're nuts! The Japanese have some nasty tricks in their wrestling repertoire." But I told the colonel that it was a deal.

"Il est d'accord!"

The colonel gave instructions to one of his staff. After a short wait, he returned, accompanied by a stocky, powerful-appearing young officer. The colonel spoke to him and during their conversation both laughed several times. I wondered what was up.

The contender, a lieutenant, was presented to us and he saluted. The colonel asked me if we'd follow him and we all walked over to a grassy plot which would serve as the ring. The lieutenant stripped to the waist.

When I saw the officer's powerful torso muscles, I told Mike, "If you want to back out, I'll tell the colonel I've changed my mind."

Mike, who was stripping, displayed a typical wrestler's build, which reassured me somewhat.

"What about it, Mike?"

"Let's go! I'm ready."

One of the officers was selected as the referee and the two opponents squared off. It was soon apparent that Mike was faster than his opponent. He moved like a cat. Each tried for a hold, but the Japanese officer was trying mainly for a crusher body hold, which Mike was avoiding. In a sudden countermove, Mike got a flying mare on him, flinging him on his back. Then they tossed one another around while off their feet, with Mike having his opponent locked in a scissors, squeezing the Japanese officer's guts. The officer got loose and managed to get to his feet, but Mike caught him with a flying tackle and he fell hard. With a jerk, Mike pulled the officer toward himself, jumped forward, and caught him in a headlock while he was still on his back. With his shoulder compressing the officer's, Mike locked his shoulders flat on the lawn. The referee tapped Mike as the winner.

"Good show, Mike!"

I approached the colonel and he unhooked the sword and handed it to me, saying, "Il a bien fait, un vrai gladiateur!"

I turned over the sword to Mike, who had already put on his shirt.

"Here it is, you lucky bastard! Most likely, wrestling is the only gem of knowledge you picked up in college." He grinned.

"Just crossed my mind, Mike. I'm not so smart either. We could both be court-martialed for this stupid stunt!"

He laughed. "I don't give a goddamn! I've got a Samurai!"

"Yes! And what the hell did I get out of this caper?"

On the way back to Thakhet, I wondered why the Japanese officer hadn't been more effective in latching a hold on Mike when the opportunity occurred. The jolly talk between him and the colonel had me bothered. "Mike, was the Japanese going all out to tie you up?"

"Now that you ask, he could have caught me several times. Why?"

"Oh, just an idle question. Forget it!"

So that was it! The colonel knew that he'd never get back to Japan with such a sought-after souvenir (all Japanese were disarmed before boarding the ships) and he evidently figured he might as well have a bit of fun over it and possibly save face before his staff. He'd outfoxed us. We'd been had!

But Mike did have his pride and joy, which he was constantly admiring. All I had was the gas for our trek to Hanoi which would be expended on our trip. I would have no souvenir or memento!

We loaded up some rations, bedding rolls, weapons, and ammo in our vehicle. The driver was ready.

I left Lieutenant Ellis in command. "Just stay around our base and, if the fighting gets too hot, take the team over to Nakhon Phanom and stay with the governor. We'll be back within three days. Keep in touch with Kunming."

Our route led east to the Vietnamese coastal road, which we hit a bit north of Hue. Then we headed north. En route, we had to cross three or four estuaries where the bridges had been destroyed by our bombers. We had to cross on native ferries that were poled and rowed so slowly that Mike and I swam across, arriving on the opposite shore before the ferries did.

At the last crossing, I spoke to one of the villagers and asked if any dangerous fish were in those waters. The ferryman had told me "Non" to that question at each crossing.

The villager pondered and then in halting French said, "Non, mais de temps en temps il y a des requins."—sometimes there are sharks!

At Dong Hoi we passed a Japanese regiment in bivouac waiting for orders to head for Siam. Farther north, we also passed a Chinese Nationalist battalion moving south. The soldiers were a depressing sight to a military man. They were coughing, spitting, and wiping their noses with their sleeves. Their uniforms were unbuttoned and dirty. They marched in poor formation and appeared fagged out.

"Mike, I'll bet if they get near the Japanese outfit we passed, they'll wind up doing coolie work for them."

He laughed. "They look piss poor."

"Yes, they're a sorry bunch!" I concluded.

A bit farther north we noticed what looked like a government agricultural station with several quite large administrative buildings. However, we observed Viet Minh troops mounting guard around them. I was curious and had the driver pull up to them to ask if the buildings were a prison. The guards told me that a group of French officers was being held there. They'd been interned there by the Japanese, who had turned them over to the Vietnamese.

I spoke to the interned officers—about seventy-five of them. They appeared in good health and they informed me that they were adequately fed and housed. They asked if I could obtain their release. I advised them that I was on my way to the China Command in Hanoi and would report their confinement.

I warned the guard commander to treat the officers well and assured him that they would be evacuated shortly. Even if I had been able to convince the commander to release the officers, there would have been the grave risk of exposing them to a massacre, since the Vietnamese were determined to be rid of the French now that Ho Chi Minh had proclaimed Vietnam an independent republic. Having the officers evacuated by representatives of the China Command, through an agreement effected with Ho's staff, was the only safe way to get them to Hanoi.

At Vinh, we picked up a Swiss national who said he owned a large farm in the neighborhood. He said he was scared of the natives because they considered him French and he wanted to get to Hanoi where he had heard there was an American headquarters.

That night we reached Hanoi and checked into the one European hotel, the Métropole. The next day I reported to General Gallagher at the China Command, Indochina headquarters. I briefed him on the southern Laotian situation and informed him of the French officers being held near Dong Hoi.

He appeared pleased. "This is the first scrap of information I've had on that whole area. No, the French are not authorized to operate in our area. About all you can do is tell them to keep south of our zone. As for the French at Dong Hoi, I'll arrange for their evacuation."

At least he'd given me something to go on to jawbone and persuade the French commanders to desist and leave.

When I got back to the hotel, Mike and our driver were waiting for me.

"Bad news, chief!"

"What the hell now?"

"The hotel clerk told me the driver claims a couple of valves were scorched on our trip and he has to get them repaired."

I asked the driver how long we'd be laid up.

"Trois ou quatre jours."

This was no good. I wanted to get going early the next day. I figured we had two choices—ask China Command for a vehicle and driver or use Mike's charm on old Ho.

"Mike, let's go to Ho's headquarters at Government House and see if we can wangle a lift. You said Ho took a shine to you."

"Sure, I'll tackle him!"

We walked to the far side of the small lake in a centrally located park where the former French governor's house stood. Mike asked to see Ho. A few of his aides spoke fair English and in a short time ushered us into Ho's large office. The louvered French doors were folded back, allowing the sun's rays to flood the room. Ho Chi Minh, in a typical white Annamite jacket and trousers, was standing alongside his desk: a small, frail-looking man with a tiny goatee. He had a fatherly look about him.

He greeted Mike in his broken English, assuring him that it was a pleasure to see him again. Mike introduced me and told him that I spoke French, whereupon he welcomed me in French and asked how long we'd been in Hanoi. I told him that we had arrived last night and had to leave as soon as possible for Thakhet, but that our car had broken down.

"Qu'est-ce que vous allez faire?"

I told him we were hoping that he could help us.

Then he smiled. "Soyez tranquille! Demain je pars pour le sud et vous deux sont invités." He was going on a trip south the next day and we could join him.

I let out a sigh of relief. "C'est très gentille de votre part. Merci."

When we got back to the hotel, a small group of the OSS China staff on a sightseeing jaunt were preparing to return to Kunming. I spotted Colonel Heffner, the station chief. I rapidly explained the situation in our operational area and stressed that I'd never received any reply to my requests for specific instructions and that I had come to Hanoi to get an opinion from General Gallagher. The colonel asked me what Gallagher said.

"He confirmed that the French should not be operating

near Tha Khet and to dissuade them from continuing their activities in our theater of operations.''

"Well, I agree, get them the hell out of there!''

"Many thanks! Wish I'd been told that before.''

That night, we dined at a French restaurant just opened since the release of the French garrison. There was a crowd of recently freed French officers and their families and some Americans but also, surprisingly, a number of Japanese officers.

Although the official surrender still hadn't taken place, there didn't appear to be any signs of animosity present. Each group enjoyed themselves. A peacetime ambience prevailed. No one would have thought that these Japanese had kept these French officers immobilized for more than four years, the last six months in actual confinement. Perhaps it was the fact that it was all over and done with, that they were safe, and, as far as the French were concerned, together with their families once more.

We were picked up at dawn by Ho's chauffeur and taken to his residence. He came out with an aide carrying a briefcase and sat alongside the driver.

"Bonjour! Avez-vous bien dormi?''

Some more pleasantries were exchanged and we started. Gradually, Ho and I started discussing the Vietnamese situation. Evidently he found me to be a sympathetic listener, because he had the car stopped and he switched seats with his aide so he could sit between Mike and me. Ho's slim hips made things roomier than his aide's broad beam—a relief.

We stopped at some of the larger towns where receptions had evidently been prepared for him. Crowds were on hand and cheered him. He was their president, acclaimed so by the Viet Minh, and he was paid due respect. We would remain by the car with the chauffeur, his aide usually hobnobbing with the reception committee. Ho addressed his people as his children and he gave the impression of a father talking to his family. From time to time, the crowd would stare at us, evidently because of something Ho had said.

I was curious about that and asked the chauffeur the first time it occurred, "Qu'est-ce qu'il a dit?''

Although he spoke some French, the chauffeur just

shrugged his shoulders to my questions regarding Ho's remarks. Finally, after several stops, I asked Ho.

He smiled and stated, "Les Americains nous montrent beaucoup de sympathie." (The Americans are very sympathetic.) He continued by declaring that the Americans with whom he had been in contact were very understanding and sympathetic to his goals in establishing an independent republic.

I told him that I was interested in his endeavors, but I didn't mention that OSS knew he was a Communist.

With that he enlarged on his sentiments toward Americans and the USA. "You are not colonizers like the Europeans. You have given Cuba its independence and you've pledged to do the same for the Philippines next year. Therefore, I trust you and hope for your economic, financial, and military aid in establishing our independence. We have been milked and exploited by the French who have occupied our country as a colony for the past seventy-five years."

"Was there any resistance to French rule during that time?" I asked.

"Of course! Naturellement! I personally preached resistance and publicized our plight all over the world for more than forty years and an underground movement has been in existence for some time—the Viet Minh."

"Then you weren't in Vietnam all that time?" I wanted to see if he'd admit that he had spent some years in the Soviet Union.

"Non! The French sûreté forced me to flee from my country although they didn't object to letting me reside in France, particularly during Blum's socialist administration."

"I've heard you worked in New York and London," I egged him on.

"Oui, and I spent some time in Moscow. But wherever I was, I kept on drawing attention to our enslavement. But let's return from my wanderings to the present. I am at the stage now where I require American guidance. I need a copy of your Declaration of Independence and your Constitution. I want to base my government on those noble documents."

"Is there a mixed political following supporting you, with the left and right of center represented?"

132

"Oui! But the mass of our people are politically ignorant. Only a small element is of left or right persuasion, but those are the most active and influential in our organization."

He wasn't prevaricating. While investigating war crimes in Hanoi on my first Indochina mission, I met some Viet Minh who were not commies but staunch nationalists. They had admitted that they supported Ho since he was the one leader capable of uniting the Vietnamese to gain independence, although they realized he was a commie.

By this time we had reached Vinh. Once more he was acclaimed, but this time by a really large crowd, since Vinh was one of the major coastal towns. After the reception, Ho said he'd have a short conference with Bao Dai, the emperor.

Bao Dai had been emperor of Annam, which included all of Vietnam, under the French. The Japanese allowed him to retain that status under the WWII Japanese-controlled French administration. But when the Japanese overthrew that administration in March 1945, Ho and his Viet Minh seized power, thus eliminating the ancient post of emperor. Therefore, Bao Dai wielded no political power, but he was still a symbol to many Vietnamese, particularly the upper class.

"The emperor is staying here temporarily. Come along! I won't be long," Ho said.

After a short walk, we approached a large, typical French colonial house and were admitted by a servant. After we were introduced, Bao Dai invited us for lunch. He was short, like most Indochinese, but stockier, with a well-rounded face. While he and his aide and Ho conversed at a separate table, Mike and I, over our bowls of rice and seafood, reflected on the lengthy conversation I had had with Ho. Since Mike's French was rudimentary, he had not understood much of it but agreed with my feeling that Ho liked us.

From what I had heard from some of the OSS section chiefs, I realized that our government policy was not to assist the French in reestablishing themselves in Indochina.

Several other aspects of what Ho had said stood out clearly in my mind. By emphasizing that we were not a colonial power or imperialists like the French and British, he implied that he trusted us. His reference to our having given Cuba its independence and our having pledged independence for the Philippines in 1946 attested to this.

Mike was a little puzzled at Ho's request for copies of our Declaration of Independence and Constitution as guidelines for an independent Vietnam, since Ho was a Communist. He could form a communist government but, of course, to do so with any chance of success, he would have to accept aid from the Soviets.

"Why doesn't he?" Mike asked.

My answer to that was that Ho evidently did not trust them. He spent years in Moscow, where he studied Marxism and underwent training as a communist agent and organizer. During that period, he had the opportunity to judge their imperialistic aims. Apparently, he feels, although a Communist, that Vietnam's future independence would be much more secure by dealing with us rather than obligating himself to the Soviets.

Ho really seemed to want U.S. assistance and support in terms of economic, financial, and military aid. And he realized that the ties or restraints we'd apply would be far less obnoxious and dangerous to his regime than that of the monolithic, imperialistic Soviets.

"How far can we trust 'Old Ho'?" Mike wondered aloud. "Suppose we furnish all the aid he requires and generally support his regime and then he dumps the Nationalists and pulls a switch to communism, wouldn't we be in a stew?"

That, of course, would be the calculated risk the West would have to take.

"It seems to me, Mike, that there are significant overriding factors that would inhibit Ho from attempting to establish a communist government. Above all, he needs our support or, as he undoubtedly realizes, the French will take military measures to reimpose their sovereignty over Vietnam. Our team's experience in southern Laos already witnessed that.

"And dumping the Nationalists, the noncommunist elements in the government he's forming from his regime would cause the United States to drop him like a hot potato. Then he would have to rely on the Soviets for support, with consequences he seems to want to avoid. Also, the French would return militarily and politically to Vietnam, but in this case supported with arms and munitions by the United States."

If the French returned as soldiers, I was sure that Ho would fight, and we knew that his people were one hundred percent behind him. That would embroil Ho in a war against the invading French—a dirty, bloody, guerrilla war. It was clear—at least to me—that at this point Ho might avoid those pitfalls by playing ball with us and obtaining independence under simpler and much more favorable conditions.

Sipping my tea, I concluded that even if his regime might be somewhat socialist-tinged, Ho would be tied to the West just as the Yugoslav-Tito administration was.

"Sounds to me as if you have it pretty well tapped. Let's hope our State Department adopts such a course," Mike responded, nibbling an oriental cookie that didn't tell one's fortune.

Our observations of the tête-à-tête between Ho and Bao was that not much headway was being made in coming to a decision.

"Ho seems pushy and Bao indecisive," I remarked.

"I've noticed that, too. They sure don't appear to be doing the tango," Mike said, grinning.

Their lack of accord was, indeed, most apparent. Evidently Ho was angling for Bao Dai's endorsement and support. I could sense Bao's dilemma over backing a known Communist even though he had been acclaimed as president, or siding with the French on whom he had been accustomed to depend for financial support, since the French would resist communism if they were able to regain their colony. Bao certainly didn't make that decision that day!

The discussion ended and I was included in a bit of chit-chat about unrelated things.

"Il faut que nous partions. Nous sommes pressés," Ho finally said. After thanking the emperor for his hospitality, we left.

As we approached Dong Hoi, we again passed the Japanese cantonment where, as I said, the Chinese column we'd seen would be doing their camp chores. Sure enough, there they were, encamped nearby and policing the Japanese area. We laughed like hell!

"Most likely they are feeding them better than the handful-of-rice ration they're used to," I remarked.

We stopped at Dong Hoi for another acclamation and continued to Hue. Again a big crowd greeted Ho and he gave them a short address. Then Ho came back to the car and informed me that he was going to stay here overnight but that he'd just arranged for a local driver to get us to our destination and then return to Hue. I thanked him for his courtesy and assistance and wished him well. We shook hands and he patted Mike on the back. "Mes amis, adieu et bonne chance!" he said and then walked away with his aide.

Our new chauffeur got into the car and we started to retrace our route until we reached the cutoff road to Thakhet. It was already quite late and the road pitch black where the rays of the headlights didn't penetrate. We broke out some rations from our packs and while we munched we talked. Mike wanted to know what Bao Dai's situation was.

I explained that, as I understood it, Bao was a flunky for the French. His family had ruled Annam for a long time. The French kept them on as figureheads, furnishing them with a comfortable stipend. And that's what Bao depended on. If he didn't side now with Ho, and the French regained their colony, he'd be comfortably taken care of for life. The French would use him as a symbolic puppet or, if they didn't, Bao would most likely wind up permanently in France on the Riviera, living the life of Riley.

However, if Bao sided with Ho and Ho won, Bao's future would be uncertain. He had to choose between a sure bet if the French returned and a question mark if he threw in with Ho.

"How the hell do you know all this?" Mike jibed.

"As soon as I got a hint that I'd get this mission, I had SI give me a quickie on history, personalities, and the current situation."

"That's more than I got when they sent me in," grumbled Mike.

"Apart from what Ho told me, the whole independence issue was sparked additionally when the Nazi-installed regime in France made a deal with the Japanese when they invaded French Indochina. The result was that the French military did not resist, hardly a shot was fired, and, in turn, the Japanese allowed Vichy to continue to administer the colony until this past March when they ousted it.''

"You mean to say the French Army didn't even try to stage a token resistance?'' Mike asked.

"Not sufficient to call it that. The French military were impotent, although not prisoners until March when the Japanese got tough and put them all in confinement. No reflection on the French Army. They had to obey Vichy's orders.

"After the Japanese ousted the French administration, they allowed Ho and his Viet Minh to take over administration and control as the head of the new regime. That set Bao adrift and he's faced with the dilemma of deciding whether to depend on the French coming back or to support Ho.''

"That accounts for the apparent lack of accord between the two at lunch,'' said Mike.

"Now you've got the drift! Bao can't make up his mind.''

It was well after midnight when we reached our little base. A few hours later, the driver took off for Hue with our thank-you note for Ho. After all, he'd been damn decent to us.

Lieutenant Ellis reported that, apart from continued French attacks, one incident had occurred during our absence. It appears that the British SOE officer stationed across the river in Siam had crossed in a launch with a French officer who evidently wanted to make contact with the French commandos in the vicinity of Thakhet. A Laotian patrol happened to be near the ferry landing in front of our quarters. When the launch was tied to the pier, the two officers started to walk along the dock toward shore. The patrol opened fire, killing the Frenchman. The British officer, with the help of some of our team, carried the body back to the launch.

I looked up Thao Pheng and asked him why the patrol didn't warn the Frenchman to turn back.

"Parce qu'ils font la guerre contre nous.''

I couldn't deny that the French were waging war against the Laotians and dropped the subject. The Frenchman had asked for it.

"Are you using the ambush tactics I outlined for you?'' I asked Thao.

"Oui! We gave the French bloody noses on several occasions and they're more cautious, but they've upped their mortar fire."

When I returned, I asked Lieutenant Ellis if the French had increased their mortar fire.

He confirmed this. "You'll witness the fireworks tonight!"

I decided that the best way to try and settle this was to arrange a parley. A boatman rowed me across to the Siamese shore, but I didn't know the location of the Britisher's pad. I contacted the governor who knew I'd gone on a trip. He said he was glad I was back because he was concerned over the nightly assaults on Thakhet, although it was in Laos. He dispatched a guide who led me to the Britisher's base close to the river. The Britisher's radio operator, an attractive young French woman in uniform, said he wouldn't be back till late.

I returned to the governor's compound and visited with him. I told him I'd been to Hanoi and that China Command had verified that the French should *not* be operating north of the 16th parallel in Vietnam and Laos.

"What is going to be done about that situation?" he asked.

"I'm going to try and arrange a parley to convince the French to withdraw."

"I wish you luck. But I understand that the British in this area are assisting them with arms and ammunition."

"I've suspected that right along and I'll address that too."

The governor also wanted to know if Ho Chi Minh had set up an independent republic, and was dismayed when I told him he had. "I would hate to have a communist Laos alongside my province," he said, gazing at me sadly.

I told him that even though Ho was a Communist, he was a Nationalist first. Moreover, there was a sizable nationalist faction supporting his movement. So I thought his ideology might be modified by their influence, but only if the United States supported him. Otherwise, I was sure he would lean on the Soviets and that influence would certainly pressure Laos.

I could see that the governor was still disturbed. However, it was time I went back to have another look-see for the British fellow. He had come back and invited me into the hut he'd set up as his living quarters.

Over a couple of gin and tonics, I asked him if he could arrange a parley with the French commando officer directing the nightly raids, since they both served the same command. He agreed and a time and locale were selected.

"Now, if the French are out of line, how about you here in Siam, which is not your theater?" he inquired.

"You're not trying to compare my visiting you or the governor to the French conducting bloody raids on Thakhet? And as long as we're on the subject, let me tell you that I have a pretty good idea of what those empty containers around here mean." There were several other huts in the little compound and the few Siamese working for the Britisher had carelessly left a few canisters lying around.

The Britisher didn't deny my inference.

"Let's drop it," he said and I left.

That night it was quite evident that the French were relying more on heavy mortar fire than on direct assault. Mike wanted to go and check on the action, but I told him to forget it. I didn't want us embroiled in any direct involvement in the hostilities. We would just pull strings from behind the scenes.

Several days later, we met the French commando officer at the appointed locale off the Savannakhet road. I had taken the precaution of having Mike and most of my team escort me as a security element. A group of at least a dozen well-armed French troopers were waiting at the fringe of the verdant forest and I was sure many more were there on call.

We lined up opposite them and a bearded, stocky officer sporting a paratrooper claret-colored beret and wearing tropical shorts stepped forward as I did. We saluted and the parley was on.

He asked me what I wanted to discuss, which of course he already knew. I was surprised at his use of the King's English.

This guy is British without a doubt! I said to myself. The British are in this hand and glove with the French. I notified him that the French had no business operating in the China Command theater and that General Gallagher and my section chief wanted them to leave.

He laughed. "What the bloody hell is so awful in our campaigning a few miles into your territory? After all, it's still French as far as we're concerned," he rebutted with his voice rising and his face starting to turn the color of his beret.

"Regardless of your sentiments, you're committing murder like a bunch of bandits. I'm requesting that you get your troops below the 16th parallel, just south of Savannakhet."

He bridled at this. It suddenly struck home that if anything nasty was intended, it would happen now. But his answer was less belligerent than I expected.

"We'll think it over."

"A final warning: If you continue operating here, I'll radio for a drop of Chinese paratroopers."

He saluted and walked back to his cohorts. I acknowledged his salute and, when I turned to walk away, I was reassured when I noted my team in skirmish line, ready for action.

When we got back to base, I explained the conversation that had taken place. "That guy was British and I can see the tie-in with the French. If the latter lose Indochina, the British fear they'll lose the Malay States and even India. They'll play ball with each other."

"Considering how easily the Japanese took over Southeast Asia, their prestige has flopped," observed Mike.

"Anyway, if the French don't pull up stakes, I'll radio for Chinese paratroopers to force them out," I said.

"Let's see what happens tonight," said Lieutenant Ellis.

That night, the commandos delivered their answer by intensifying their nightly mortar fire. The crunch of exploding shells was nearer our base than before.

I had the radio operator encode a message describing the situation and also referring to Colonel Heppner's remark.

The response was simple. "Continue observation of situation."

We were just wasting our time. They were not going to do a goddamn thing!

The next morning, I called in Thao Pheng and advised him that I had requested Chinese paratroopers to straighten out the commandos but couldn't promise my request would be acted upon. He was a bit dismayed. I wanted to move the team over to the governor's compound across the river because I was concerned that the commandos would zero in on us. We were the only thorn in their side. But I didn't want to discourage Thao completely since it could weaken his resolve to resist.

Before Thao left, I again inquired how he fared in the way of arms and ammunition. He responded that the Japanese kept him supplied.

Once more, the nightly assault began and several mortar rounds almost zeroed in on our residence. The radio operator, on his late-night radio schedule, brought me a decoded message. It directed that we move over to Nakhon Phanom and await evacuation orders.

In the morning, I had Thao Pheng report back and told him we were going to stay with the governor across the river and await an evacuation plane. However, to cheer him up a bit over our departure, we left a good portion of our medical and, except for our army rations, the food supplies as well. I told him I'd cross over daily to see him until we left for the plane.

The governor and his staff furnished us quarters and a few servants to take care of the housekeeping. We had our meals with the governor and his staff and enjoyed the various Siamese dishes. Rice was the staple and was served with or in most dishes.

The governor and his staff were sorry to hear that we wouldn't be with them for long. They really enjoyed our association and camaraderie.

"Your parley didn't succeed," the governor exclaimed as we listened after dinner to the rattle of small arms and the crunch of mortar shells exploding across the river.

"No, I didn't get the backing and support I requested to sustain my demands on the commandos," I said bitterly.

"But even though you're leaving, the resistance to the French assaults to retake southern Laos is not diminishing," he said ruefully.

I sensed that he wanted my opinion on the eventual outcome of the situation. "I think the Laotians and, of course, the Vietnamese will resist all French attempts to regain their colonial mastery. They want to be as independent as Siam. Ho Chi Minh had expressed it quite pithily to me: 'If the

French return as merchants, they're welcome. But if they return as soldiers, we'll fight.' "

"In that case, we can expect violence and chaos over there—something I don't look forward to since it could create border problems. I say that because I believe the French will make an all-out effort."

"Governor," I said, "you've hit it on the head. Be prepared to handle refugees."

"Well, to get on a more pleasant subject, how about going on a vulture hunt? We've got too many around here."

"Excellent! It'll give my team a chance to blow off steam."

Before we started out the next day, however, I had an early-morning meeting with Thao Pheng.

"Nothing has changed," Thao said. "They haven't stopped attacking."

"Just keep on using the tactics I showed you. If you bloody them enough, their native troops will slack off. I don't think there are more than a dozen French and British commandos with them."

"Although we have a reputation of not being as warlike as the Annamites, we will fight to stay free."

"Bravo! Good luck!" I concluded, sensing that it might be the last time I'd see him.

The governor and his brother, who was custom's director, led the hunt into a nearby forest full of vultures that were huge and very sluggish. As we approached, they flew from tree to tree.

"These birds are easy targets," I said.

"I know, but we want to thin them out." The governor then started banging away with an old, well-worn shotgun.

"OK! Here we go!" I signaled to Mike and the rest of the team to join in. When we had cleaned out that batch of birds, we moved farther into the forest until we stumbled on another flock and again gave our carbines a workout.

The governor tried my carbine and evidently was impressed with it. When he handed it back, he smilingly joked, "World War II is over, you won't need it anymore."

"I guess not," I said. "When we leave, I don't think my headquarters will mind if I give it to you with a thousand rounds and a half-dozen magazines."

He was as delighted as a little kid.

When we got back, the radio operator who had stayed behind to be on hand for his radio schedule handed me a decoded message. "That's our flight ticket," he said.

And so it was! We had to rendezvous at an auxiliary airfield at Udon, about 150 miles almost due east, within a bracket of three to five days.

I arranged with the Siamese governor to have a truck take us there and he wired the governor of Udon, alerting him to expect us.

That evening, we had a gala dinner with the Siamese governor and sampled his champagne. He and his staff were genuinely sorry we were leaving. We'd been a very compatible group.

"Governor, we've enjoyed your hospitality and I'm sorry we can't amply repay you. But you do inherit my carbine and ammo plus all our remaining medical supplies. Our stay in Siam with you will always be a cherished memory to us."

"Americans will always be welcome here," he assured me. And we clinked our glasses against a backdrop orchestrated by the martial tune of musketry and mortar fire.

Escorted by the governor's brother, we left the next morning. Sitting in the bed of the truck, we relaxed and discussed all the aspects of our mission.

"This is a hell of a note to have us bug out without any attempt to alleviate the local situation," Mike said angrily.

"I can't understand why SI completely disregarded all our references to it," Ellis chimed in.

"It's been bothering me since I indicated Colonel Heppner's attitude toward the whole incident," I observed. "After considering all their options, I've concluded that SI decided not to involve the OSS in what could develop into a heated dispute between the China and Southeast Asia commands. SI has taken the easy way out. They're most likely justifying their position on the basis that only a very small force was conducting those renegade activities."

"I guess you've figured it out," said Mike with resignation in his voice.

We all nodded affirmatively. But the sour taste of that experience never left me.

The governor of Udon province, a retired Siamese army

officer, extended all the amenities at his disposal and we enjoyed his hospitality. Several days later, the plane arrived and evacuated us.

When we reported in at our Kunming headquarters, we were notified that OSS had been directed to disband on 1 October, several weeks prior to our arrival. OSS was moving out and we were among the last teams to be called in. I rendered a full report on the mission and Lieutenant Ellis turned in his intelligence report.

# CHAPTER 8

---

# The Quiescent Period

A few days later, we were flown to Calcutta and, after a two-week wait, we were herded onto a small liberty ship. Twenty-seven confining, boring days later, we landed at Tacoma, Washington, and flew on to Washington, D.C. At OSS headquarters, I was handed my reassignment orders to the Army Counter Intelligence Corps (CIC). So ended my active association with OSS. The era of operating unfettered on your own—some called it freewheeling—in the arena of unconventional warfare was over, but for how long?

I realized that although OSS had been deactivated, the employment of unconventional warfare would continue just as it had throughout the centuries—if not on one part of the globe then on another. What concerned me was whether or not the vacuum left by blindly dismantling an organization that had proved itself so indispensable as an essential component of total warfare would be properly filled. I was convinced that there was a requirement for an organization such as OSS preferably within the military—the Army. I had noted that often logistic and air support for OSS had not been given a high level of priority by the military. Rather its priority was on the low end of the scale. If there were an abundance of what had been requested or requisitioned on hand, OSS got a break; otherwise it didn't. Also, better coordination in planning and operations as well as an appreciation of such an organization's scope of operations and capabilities would further the overall effort against the common enemy. An organized unconventional warfare setup could prevent the bypassing of the military, communication-wise, by a private system.

Such a UW force, trained and ready to operate, with an established operational base stockpiled with the arms, munitions, and commo equipment needed for the initial organization of indigenous resistance/guerrilla movements, could be as essential as any of the combat arms—armor, infantry, artillery—that comprise our arsenal.

There are two overriding reasons for this contention. Organized on the team concept of OSS, such teams must be infiltrated at the outset of hostilities. At that time, the enemy's internal security agencies and forces and those of its satellites are not completely organized or deployed. This affords the infiltrating teams maximum mobility and reasonable security to organize the resistance/guerrilla potential. Furthermore, at that time the potential manpower sought by the teams was still available since even early mobilization would not have siphoned off a significant number.

A third factor is also involved: language fluency and area knowledge. Although personnel can be taught the basics of UW in a three-month crash course, it takes at least a year to teach a foreign language to the point where one is operationally language capable. Area studies also require considerable time.

Therefore, if a unit were to start from scratch after hostilities had commenced and produce top-notch operatives, it couldn't initiate effective operations in less than one year.

Until my reassignment to the 11th Airborne Division in the spring of 1950, I had time to satisfy my strong interest in the long history of unconventional warfare. This was sparked by the formation in 1947 of the CIA, which adopted the heritage of the Special Intelligence branch of OSS. Although there was also a covert mission included in the field of resistance movements and, to some extent, in guerrilla warfare, the need still existed in my book for the Army to adopt the total heritage left by the Special Operations branch of OSS for the conduct of large-scale, global, UW operations. I felt fully justified in that opinion.

A bit of intermittent research and perusal of pertinent British, French, and American UW reference books and articles revealed an exciting record reaching back through the centuries. In fact, unconventional warfare undoubtedly goes back further than written history; most likely it's as old as war itself.

This ancient but still-current practice had bloodied armies and caused them to stumble and falter, disrupted well-planned military timetables, and diverted excessively large forces and equipment from their conventional combat role. In spite of always being a thorn in the side of the military, until WWII, with a few exceptions, UW has been regarded as a sideshow of no great consequence. To the orthodox, traditional soldier, it was something slimy, underhanded, illegal, and ungentlemanly. It did not fit in the honor code of that profession of arms.

The earliest trace of UW that I could find went back to the biblical period of David, the warrior king of the Israelites, who utilized it against the Philistines. Still in biblical times, but at a later period, the Israelites again used UW against their Roman conquerors although without success. It is even recorded in Greek mythology in the legend of the Trojan horse. In the fourteenth century, it was embraced by the Bulgars in their revolt against their Byzantine rulers. The ruling Turkish sultan supported the Bulgars in their rebellion. This made a significant impact on the future relationship between resistance/guerrilla movements and supporting external powers.

External support is an essential ingredient in assuring the success of a resistance/guerrilla movement, whether its goal is to gain liberation from foreign occupation or freedom from its own government which it considers autocratic or oppressive. However, since the Bulgar experience, in which they and the Turks shared the benefit, that relationship has altered. Gradually, as the centuries passed, the supporting power obtained most of the benefits and, as a corollary, the control and thrust of these movements passed into its hands. This is exemplified by the methods of the Soviets and their surrogates in spreading their ideology, doctrine, and control in both hemispheres.

In the fifteenth century in the Far East, we find that under the Annamite Le dynasty, after ten centuries of repeated uprisings by resistance movements the Chinese oppressors were finally expelled. Then, in the mid-seventeen hundreds on the other side of the globe, the French incited and supported the Indian tribes to conduct guerrilla warfare against the British colonies in North America during the French and Indian Wars. Shortly thereafter, following the "shot heard around the world" at Lexington, our Concord farmers for one memorable day conducted guerrilla warfare when they ambushed and harassed the redcoats' withdrawal. As our revolution against the British continued, there were some American leaders whose bands conducted a campaign utilizing guerrilla tactics. These were Francis Marion (the Swamp Fox), Andrew Pickens, and Thomas Sumter. But since they led regular troops, their activities could not be classed as guerrilla warfare. Only partisans, irregular troops, or groupings of un-uniformed civilians conducting combat operations behind the lines are classed as guerrillas.

Napoleon's armies, those that invaded and occupied Spain between 1807 and 1813, so provoked the population that they organized a national resistance movement and conducted guerrilla warfare against his lines of communications and supply depots, thus forcing the French to redeploy large forces to protect their lifeline back to the French border. Therefore, they never were able to employ their full strength against Wellington's British expeditionary force. In the end, Napoleon had to withdraw his exhausted armies without achieving any of his political or military objectives, and having sustained a loss of half of his troops.

Toward the latter period of the foregoing Peninsular campaign, Napoleon again experienced the impact of guerrilla warfare. During his retreat from Moscow in 1812, the Russian partisans sank their fangs into his half-starved and -frozen Grande Armée when they swarmed around his flanks and rear like wolf packs. Had it not been for the personal bravery and leadership of Marshal Ney, commander of the rearguard, the partisans might have devoured Napoleon's army.

Back to North America: During the Civil War, some of the Confederate cavalry commanders, such as John Mosby in northern Virginia, used guerrilla tactics very effectively. But it was William Quantrill who actually conducted guerrilla warfare in Missouri and Kansas, since he led irregulars.

Again in Europe, during the Franco-Prussian War, from 1870 to 1871, the guerrilla phase of UW once more played a significant role, without preventing defeat, however, since the guerrillas had no external support. The Francs-Tireurs inflicted severe casualties on the German invaders to the extent that Marshal von Moltke ordered all prisoners shot who were not fully uniformed and led by regular officers.

At the turn of the century, the Boers, fighting against the British, conducted extensive, coordinated guerrilla warfare under Smuts and Botha. And during the same period, the U.S. Army carried out a long campaign against Aguinaldo's Filipino and Moro guerrillas.

Pancho Villa, originally a cattle rustler in northern Mexico, started conducting guerrilla warfare in support of presidential aspirants from 1912 to 1920. In 1916, he raided Columbus, New Mexico. He eluded a pursuing U.S. Army expeditionary force under General Pershing which withdrew when President Carranza, whom Villa had previously chased out of Mexico City, voiced objections.

From 1912 to 1933, with the exception of 1926, U.S. Marines were on duty in Nicaragua to maintain law and order. From 1927, Cesar Sandino conducted a guerrilla campaign against the Marines and was instrumental in effecting their departure.

World War I (1914–1918) was the scene of a thrilling and most notable example of guerrilla warfare. The legendary Col. T. E. Lawrence encouraged, supported, and helped Feisal al Hussein lead his Arab guerrilla forces in isolating and harassing large Turkish forces in the Mecca-Medina area of present Saudi Arabia. This so weakened the Turks that they crumbled under a single, decisive blow by a British Army under General Allenby.

Focusing again on the Far East, from the late 1920s until he gained control of China in 1949, Mao Tse-tung led a vast guerrilla army to victory over the Kuomintang (Nationalists). Based on his lengthy experience in the total field of UW and the volumes he wrote, he established a reputation as the outstanding authority and pundit on the subject.

In 1940, when the Nazis overran Denmark, Norway, France, Belgium, Holland, and Luxembourg in World War II, the indomitable British Prime Minister Sir Winston

Churchill determined that an agency initially would be formed to unleash UW in those countries. Little did he realize the proportions it would assume, the magnitude of the forces it would generate, or its future impact on world events. And when he was asked by the chief of that agency, dubbed Special Operations Executive (SOE), what his prime mission was, Churchill responded in his gravelly voice, "Set Europe ablaze!"

That quotation set off a chain of events that would have a decided effect on the conduct of the war and would afford UW a modicum of recognition and support from the military.

In 1941, President Roosevelt followed suit and directed Col. (later Maj. Gen.) Bill Donovan to form an agency for the collection of worldwide intelligence. It was dubbed the office of Coordinator of Information (COI) and after the Japanese assault on Pearl Harbor, when the U.S. entered the conflict, the mission was expanded to include all aspects of UW. In the summer of 1942, it became the Office of Strategic Services (OSS). SOE and OSS coordinated their clandestine and covert activities after setting up operational bases in Europe, North Africa, India, Burma, and, by OSS independently, in China. Thus, UW would be conducted on a massive scale and on a global basis.

In Europe alone, General Eisenhower declared that the contribution of the resistance movement had been equivalent to that of fifteen infantry divisions. He based his remark on the results obtained primarily by the French resistance movement which was developed through the operations conducted by the Allied clandestine and covert agencies.

Starting in 1940, SOE and the French Bureau Central de Renseignements et Action (BCRA) infiltrated agents to guide and assist local organizers in developing resistance groups and operating their component Intelligence, sabotage, escape and evasion, and propaganda networks. By 1944, guerrilla groups in many areas started to be formed and armed. As the invasion period neared, as we have seen, the Jedburgh teams were infiltrated to exploit the guerrilla phase to the maximum extent.

I have already spoken of my individual work with OSS during World War II, but at this point it is pertinent to summarize the larger operation. For four years prior to the Normandy invasion, valuable intelligence had been collected and submitted to SHAEF, which information figured heavily in the formulation of the final invasion plans. More than five thousand Allied pilots had been rescued by the escape and evasion nets. Sabotage of enemy lines of communications and supply lines had gone on continuously as well as sabotage, both active and passive, against plants and factories producing war material for the Germans. Then, with the receipt of the invasion signal, all activity was maximized to prevent the Germans from concentrating all needed forces to resist the invasion. At least six divisions were delayed during the critical period. Armored units, forced to move by road rather than rail, arrived not only later than scheduled, but in no condition to fight. Furthermore, sizable enemy forces had to be diverted to resist the guerrillas and secure the rear areas. And, lastly, severe casualties were inflicted on the Germans.

Most of the French population was sympathetic and helpful to the Resistance. But of the two percent that were actively engaged in the Resistance, 100,000 people were killed conducting those activities as well as by enemy reprisals.

The entire operation was a classic example of the maxim that guerrilla warfare is the final and culminating expression of a successful resistance movement.

OSS and SOE were also involved in supporting guerrilla operations in Yugoslavia and Greece. Notably, Tito's forces were responsible for diverting more than two dozen German divisions attempting to suppress them, thereby preventing the Germans from gaining complete control of Yugoslavia.

The Russians, anticipating a German invasion, had established supply caches to support and sustain partisans in conducting guerrilla warfare and a scorched-earth program. Due to the surprisingly rapid advance of the enemy, only a limited partisan organizing effort was possible. Therefore, only in favorable guerrilla areas were partisans organized and trained.

Their operations at first were held at small-unit levels against lines of communication. In 1942, guerrilla-trained Russian Army officers and technical personnel were infiltrated to the partisans and, by 1943, large groups had been developed and organized under a centralized control staff of the Soviet High Command.

The partisans conducted operations on a huge scale. At

times, a number of groups up to 10,000 strong would be united for major operations. Their impact on the German rear areas was staggering. More than 250 locomotives and 1400 railway cars were destroyed. As many as 1350 assaults on all forms of transportation were reported in one month. The Germans, after doubling the number of rear-area security divisions, still had to commit five additional divisions for antiguerrilla operations in 1943. In one night, just prior to the Russian offensive against the German Central Army Group, 10,500 demolitions were effected by the partisans. This was accomplished successfully in spite of more than 80,000 enemy security personnel in that sector.

The overall contribution of the partisans was of immense proportions. The Red Army might not have been able to stave off the German onslaught without them.

In Asia, OSS was also quite prominent. Its 101 Detachment conducted a large, effective operation in Burma, where OSS organized more than ten thousand Kachin tribesmen into large guerrilla groups against the Japanese invaders. Due largely to the guerrillas' effectiveness, the Japanese were forced to abandon Burma. During the Japanese retreat, the Kachins inflicted tremendous casualties, turning it into a rout. (They also furnished guides and flank protection for Merrill's Marauders.)

In China, OSS also organized and trained guerrillas and conducted fairly extensive operations against the Japanese in support of the Nationalists (Kuomintang), but OSS had little success in coordinating with the communist Chinese. As mentioned previously, OSS did have a few teams in Indochina, but it was only a small effort.

With the return of the French to Indochina in 1946, guerrilla warfare flared up again. When the Japanese army invaded Indochina in 1941, the French army did not resist. Just as the Vichy government in France collaborated with the Nazis, so did the French in Indochina. They surrendered control of their colony to the Japanese and supplied them with rice, coal, rubber, and other raw materials. This humiliation of France by an Asian nation destroyed the image of white, colonial invincibility. The Viet Minh were more determined than ever not to surrender their recently won independent status.

During the same postwar period, unconventional warfare, fostered by a Chinese minority, cropped up in Malaya.

In the Philippines, the Hukbalahap were conducting a guerrilla campaign against the government. By 1949, the Chinese Nationalist armies were sufficiently weakened and demoralized to afford Mao Tse-tung's guerrilla forces the opportunity to go on the offensive as a conventional army and drive them off the mainland, forcing them to take refuge on Formosa.

Unconventional warfare was definitely a weapon that continued to be employed. It was a tool of dissidents regardless of their cause.

Its profound influence would continue unabated throughout the years to alter the military, political, and ideological posture of numerous small nations and create friction between the major powers. This friction in many instances is due to Soviets using this medium to spread their doctrines and gain control. But beyond that, on reflection, UW had proved itself during WWII as a companion of conventional warfare—a necessary supplement whenever the employment of conventional forces would not be feasible or would be embarrassing. I wondered when it would obtain full recognition by the military leaders of the great powers.

# CHAPTER 9

## In the UW Saddle Again

In early 1951, while on duty in Korea with the 187th Airborne Regimental Combat Team, I was reassigned to the Army Psychological Warfare (Psy War) staff.

I had practically no experience with the inner workings of this specialty except for a superficial exposure during my Jedburgh mission, when we had spread rumors, through our intelligence network, to raise the hopes and morale of the population.

How come I was selected for that job—a job better suited to a guy with journalistic or literary experience and talents? I'm not suited for dreaming up propaganda tracts and scenarios, I kept repeating to myself. In fact, I resented being pulled out of combat to do a desk job. But the die had been cast. The system was impersonal. Supposedly, one served where he was most needed.

A bit apprehensively, I reported to Brig. Gen. Robert McClure, chief of the Army Psy War staff. He greeted me with a smile.

"Welcome aboard! I know how you feel, being suddenly parted from a combat role in the 187th, but I'm sure you'll feel better about it after learning the reason."

He then explained that as General Eisenhower's Psy War chief, he had frequently coordinated such operations with the OSS Psy War element. And through this contact, he had become aware of the operations conducted by the OSS Special Operations branch and was deeply impressed. Shortly after the war ended, he decided to do what he could to influence the War Department to incorporate such an organization into the Army.

"General, since serving in OSS, I've always hoped that I'd get the opportunity to pitch for that."

"Well, you now have it. Give it all you've got. So far, the staff consists of only Lt. Col. Russ Volckmann, but I expect to get additional qualified officers to assist you. You'll find that Volckmann is a ball of fire, a real spark plug. He's already got things rolling with a couple of high-powered studies that are attracting considerable interest. Furthermore, he is extremely articulate. Your office is across the hall—the Special Operations Division."

After inquiring if I had my family quartered, he warned me we'd have to work carefully and not step on toes, since there was not only apathy about a UW army capability, but also actual resistance to elite special units. He concluded our interview by telling me that he was depending on Volckmann and me as the key men on the staff and that Volckmann would brief me.

When I walked into our two-room office, I noticed a plump young woman banging away on a typewriter. She looked up and smiled.

"As soon as I start scribbling, you'll have lots more ammunition for that machine gun of yours," I greeted her.

She laughed good-naturedly. "With any more work, this gadget will smoke."

At another desk was a slim, pale-faced lieutenant colonel who looked up as I entered.

"I'm Aaron Bank and I'm sure you're Volckmann."

"Just call me Russ," he responded with a smile.

He briefed me on McClure. Following WWII, McClure had assignments in other fields that were not connected with the Army General Staff where he could have participated directly and officially in the deliberations concerning the future staff control and coordination of Psy War or UW operations.

McClure had been director of Information Control in the U.S.-occupied zone of West Germany. Then, starting in 1947 he held the assignment of chief of the New York office of the

Civil Affairs Division. In early 1949, he was switched from staff duty to become assistant division commander of the 4th Infantry Division. Nevertheless, his advice and opinions on matters relating to Psy War were requested continually by the Army General Staff. McClure found this stimulating since he enjoyed having his expertise in his specialized field recognized.

McClure's next assignment was based on several factors. Since the end of World War II, Psy War had been a staff responsibility first of the Army G-2 and then G-3, to which arrangement McClure strenuously objected. He felt that Psy War was classed as a minor responsibility by the G-3 staff and therefore received scant attention. This opinion was supported by the Army's minimal capability in this area at the outbreak of hostilities in Korea.

McClure insisted that psychological warfare be put in the hands of an independent special staff. His rationale was that the chief of a general staff at Army level would have direct access to the Army Chief of Staff, whereas a subdivision chief would be shortstopped by the chief of a special staff. Presumably, McClure speculated that he had the inside track to the post of chief of that staff in the event his influence bore fruit.

Following staff recommendations to the Army Chief of Staff, it was finally decided to create a small Psy War subdivision within G-3, much to the chagrin of General McClure. But shortly thereafter, evidently responding to the pressure applied by Secretary of the Army Frank Pace, who agreed with McClure's concepts and was a strong proponent of Psy War and UW, General Bolte, the G-3, reversed gears. He submitted a recommendation urging that both Psy War and UW be transferred to an independent Psy War special staff.

This was a windfall for McClure. Although he had not been plugging for UW to be incorporated into a projected Psy War staff, he had intended to do so after it was established. His pitch initially was only for his specialty—Psy War.

With the Secretary of the Army increasing the pressure supporting Bolte's recommendation, the organization and proposed personnel strength for the staff were approved with dispatch by the Army Chief of Staff on I September 1950. There was no need to search for a qualified chief for that new staff. The indispensable McClure was waiting in the wings. As he surmised, he indeed did have the inside track.

Although approved as independent, the new staff had remained within G-3 while it was being organized and it wasn't until 15 January 1950 that it became a bona fide independent special staff: Office of the Chief of Psychological Warfare (OCPW). On that date, the infant was nudged from the womb of the G-3 division and the umbilical cord was cut.

At the time, McClure was not immersed sufficiently in UW to realize that eventually it would supersede Psy War. That Psy War had the leading role as far as he was concerned was further evidenced by the small number of personnel assigned to the Special Operations branch of his staff.

Though McClure's new organization was divided into three branches—Psy War, covert deception, and Special Operations—it was entitled Psychological Warfare. According to the special regulations outlining its organization and functions, OCPW was charged with formulating and developing plans for the Army in Psy War *and* UW. The thrust was on Psy War, but Special Operations was at least in the running.

Russ's briefing thus gave me an excellent picture of the developments since World War II in respect to the emergence of OCPW. McClure was certainly a dedicated and highly motivated proponent of Psy War and he seemed fully prepared to support the project which included an unconventional warfare Army unit. All his expertise, however, was in Psy War. This made me realize that Russ and I had a tremendous task ahead of us.

Then began what turned out to be a veritable ordeal of Sisyphus. I began by getting from Russ all available material concerning UW since OSS folded.

"We've got copies of memos, studies, Tables of Organization and Equipment from G-3 plans, which will give you some idea of Army thinking and efforts in this area," Russ responded to my request.

I pored through this mass of letters, studies, and memoranda in our files and noted with dismay the lack of understanding and the confusion concerning UW, not only in reference to missions, concept, and operations, but also concerning types of units and staff control.

The opening round to establish a military UW capability was

fired by Secretary of War Robert Patterson in late 1946. He deplored the fact that no action had been initiated within the War Department staff to develop a wartime airborne reconnaissance capability. He referred to the successful utilization of reconnaissance agents by OSS. He was referring really not only to Intelligence agents and radio operators dropped by OSS but also to the Jedburgh teams and the thirty-man Operational Groups. In response to his directive, Army Ground Forces (AGF) was instructed to prepare a study on the desirability and organization of airborne reconnaissance units.

In early 1947, the War Department General Staff received this study which recommended setting up an experimental unit of six officers and thirty-five enlisted men. The G-2 (Intelligence Division of the General Staff) deemed such units essential in wartime and suggested such units be maintained in peacetime to develop techniques and doctrines of employment and that the same be taught in appropriate Army schools. AGF was then directed to develop tactics, techniques, training, and a Table of Organization and Equipment (TO&E) for submission to the War Department. When the time came to activate the program, the necessary personnel spaces would be provided.

By the middle of 1948, AGF was in contact with Col. Ray Peers, former commander of OSS Detachment 101, seeking advice on the organization of an airborne recon company which they had named Ranger Group, since there was a Ranger precedent within the Army.

The completed TO&E of the Ranger Group circulated through Army Field Forces (AFF), formerly AGF. That did not eradicate the confusion concerning the title and organization of the unit. Matters were further aggravated by the assigned missions which included both Ranger and OSS concepts. Evidently Peers had made the AFF contact officers aware of the broad scope of UW which inspired, or at least sufficiently influenced, them to include, in addition to strategic, clandestine intelligence, all the aspects of UW, thus considerably expanding the unit's responsibilities.*

The Ranger Group of approximately 250 officers and men

---

*See Alfred H. Paddock, Jr., *U.S. Army Special Warfare, Its Origins* (Washington, D.C.: National Defense University Press, 1982), 71–75.

was to be attached to Army groups or field armies. Its broadened capabilities would include the conduct of surprise raids, field sabotage in the enemy's rear areas, dissemination of propaganda, reconnaissance, espionage (by employing indigenous agents), support of guerrilla forces, and control of escape and evasion in strategic areas. But this combination of Ranger and OSS missions was not compatible with the standards, concepts, and training of either. The Rangers were strictly short-term, shallow-penetration units, whereas OSS had long-term, much more complex, strategic capabilities. And there was the rub!

Neither the Jedburghs nor the Operational Groups performed tactical missions for any conventional forces. The only exception might have been during a final linkup phase, when their area was overrun by friendly forces. In such instances, they cooperated with conventional units by furnishing intelligence and directing their guerrilla forces to furnish flank protection and/or to reduce by-passed enemy elements. They were always under direct control of OSS operational headquarters in Europe, with their own communications facilities. OSS did have liaison with General Eisenhower's Supreme Allied Headquarters (SHAEF) and direct communications with its Washington top echelon. The only close connection it had with conventional forces was through small, intelligence-collection detachments at field army level that infiltrated agents—both indigenous personnel and defectors—through the lines to gather intelligence. But nevertheless, the detachments were under the direct control of their OSS base headquarters.

Even though the Ranger Group was supposed to have UW and Ranger capabilities, that was an organizational impossibility for a unit with the limited strength of 250 officers and men. Being under the control of a tactical force not concerned about strategic operations would relegate the group's employment to direct support for raids and reconnaissance. Thus, whatever UW capability the Ranger Group possessed would be completely submerged.

The entire project foundered. A year and a half had been wasted as well as countless man-hours of staff activity. And above all, the Army still had no UW capacity. There were OSS veterans on active duty, but only one—Colonel Peers—

was approached, and then evidently his recommendations were not followed.

This obvious lack of staff officers trained in UW convinced me on the spot that one of our goals should be the preparation of a UW staff officers' course to be taught at a Special Forces Center.

With the field open for proposals, another attempt, this time initiated by the Army G-3 division, also fizzled. But the study it generated added fuel to heat up the UW pot, although not to the boiling point.

The study explored the desirability and feasibility of offering instruction in service schools in activities which would support resistance groups in the conduct of guerrilla warfare. Its recommendations were: to provide up to one day's instruction on this complicated subject (a bare scratching of the surface) in appropriate schools; to continue studying these activities; and to determine any requirement for the organization of a Special Operations company. However, a closing statement cautioned that action on the latter recommendation be held in abeyance until the Joint Chiefs of Staff (JCS) had reached a decision on the establishment of a proposed Guerrilla Warfare Corps. It had also stressed that such operations had potential as a powerful supplement to conventional warfare that should not be disregarded.

A pattern noticeably was evolving in that each study focused on the need for instruction in UW and the requirement for a peacetime organization prepared to conduct UW operations in wartime.

Influenced by Patterson's initial attempt to prod the Army into developing a wartime UW capability, coupled with the Army staff's resulting activity to address that demand, the JCS flexed its muscles and initiated studies to establish guidance and policy. These studies, which broached the organization of a Guerrilla Warfare Corps among other considerations, terminated in mid-1948.

Based on these studies, a position paper was presented to the Secretary of Defense in which the JCS expressed its attitude in reference to covert UW operations. Some of the most significant recommendations were that the government should develop a capability to support resistance/guerrilla movements in peace and war; that the CIA's limited covert operations could be expanded in order to support resistance/ guerrilla movements; that the JCS should be authorized to conduct such operations; and that the CIA should be charged with the responsibility for the conduct of all covert UW operations in peacetime and the military in wartime.

But the position paper refrained completely from supporting the establishment during peacetime of a Guerrilla Warfare Corps or of any type of UW unit within the military. Compelled by the military's inherent reluctance to be associated with any direct participation in covert UW operations, the paper ventured only so far as to recommend that selected military, CIA, and State Department personnel receive instruction in the required subjects at Army schools.

There was no mention of providing for a permanent headquarters to plan for, organize, equip, maintain at least a minimum standard of training, and to control and direct the individuals' operations in the event of hostilities. The individuals involved were to be returned to their respective services, after the minimal training provided, to be on call to conduct UW operations if required. Therefore, a manpower pool would be available but without the means or effective capability to enable it to function.

The JCS had flexed its muscles, but it was only paying lip service. It apparently was fearful of what it perceived to be the stigma of having the military accused of engaging in subrosa, cloak-and-dagger activities in the event of disclosure. The JCS dared to put its toes into what it considered to be a murky UW pool of obscured depth, but it didn't have the fortitude to plunge in. In essence, the buck was passed to the CIA.

Noting the implied reluctance of the JCS to assume a meaningful UW role, the CIA started staking its claim to fill the void. Established in 1947, the CIA was young, cocky, and ambitious.

Possibly influenced by the JCS attitude expressed while its position paper was under preparation, the National Security Council (NSC) made the obvious decision. In mid-1948, it expanded the CIA charter, which already charged the CIA with the conduct of covert Psy War, to include the conduct of UW in support of resistance/guerrilla movements.

This contributed to the unspoken desire of the CIA to take

over a military wartime role as well. If the Department of Defense hewed to the JCS position, there would not be any UW organization in the military prepared for wartime operations. That would be all the ammunition needed to justify the desired role

Not much time had elapsed when the CIA, after forming its Office of Policy Coordination (OPC) to handle its expanded covert UW operations, went on the offensive in quest of its goal. This raised the hackles of the Army staff who had not thrown in the towel. Resentfully, the staff responded by recommending that the Secretary of the Army object to a CIA report inferring that to prevent confusion and overlap with two agencies operating in the same field—covert Psy War and covert UW operations—the CIA should be the sole operating agency at all times.

But Secretary of the Army Royall had his own ideas concerning this matter. He announced, naively, that the Army was not to engage in covert UW operations or to acknowledge any ongoing activity in this area—a shocker to the Army.

However, with the CIA maneuvering to take over the whole show and the Army staff's fuming resentment thereto, the Secretary of Defense became aroused. He directed the JCS to get back in the act and reexamine its position on unconventional warfare.

The resultant study, prepared by a JCS committee, identified target areas with a resistance/guerrilla potential. These areas were primarily in eastern Europe and, to a lesser degree, in the Far East. The study concluded with the recommendation that the JCS should continue to be responsible for policy planning in unconventional warfare, within the military, and that the Army should be the prime operator, particularly for guerrilla warfare, in support of resistance/guerrilla groups.

Hopefully, this would encourage the Army to redouble its effort to overcome the doubt and confusion then existing that was hindering it from assuming its UW role.

But as things stood during 1949, only the Office of Policy Coordination (OPC) of the CIA was actually developing a covert UW capability. It was assembling the field personnel to conduct covert operations. Meanwhile, the Army was still proposing but not developing anything tangible. Army plans were still in the scribbling, paper-shuffling stage. As a result, the OPC had the deck stacked.

Based on these facts and the progress the CIA was making in compliance with its broad charter, the OPC requested assistance from the Army in obtaining a training base, logistic support, and training assistants. This request was honored but the OPC insisted that this was not a one-way show. The Army would also benefit because the specialized training would brush off on the personnel functioning as training assistants. These assistants, the OPC claimed, would develop into an UW training cadre for the Army.

Nevertheless, this hint of reciprocity did not pertain to the question of how the wartime responsibility for UW would be shifted to the Army. It remained a vague area that I realized would lead to jurisdictional squabbles of direct interest to our Special Operations branch of OCPW.

Around mid-1950, another proposal was tossed into the hopper contained in a letter to the Department of the Army composed by a former OSS/OG officer. It suggested the formation of a separate force of division strength composed of aliens from the Soviet satellite countries of Europe who were still residing in refugee camps in West Germany. They would be organized as an infantry division.* In essence, it would be a U.S. foreign legion. The only remote connection it would have to UW was that it was to be composed of aliens. The prevailing consensus was to utilize foreigners for the conduct of UW—not conventional—warfare.

After a short staff scramble, it was determined that if the Lodge Bill, which would permit aliens to enlist, passed, it would furnish only 2500 to 3000 men. Furthermore, Congress would not tolerate a separate, large alien contingent—a foreign legion—in peacetime. Amusingly enough, most of the discussion centered on the question of how the aliens would be sworn in, in the event enlistments could be effected. Not being citizens, the aliens would not be able to take the required oath to defend and uphold the Constitution. The dilemma was resolved brilliantly: Have them take an oath to the division just as French foreign legionnaires do to the le-

---

*An infantry division at that time consisted of approximately 15,000 men.

gion. However the entire exercise became academic, since the whole notion was scratched.

Annoyingly, the Army remained unable to visualize the type of organization which would be properly suited for preparing in peacetime to execute a wartime UW role, thus further enhancing OPC's dominant position.

Toward the end of my perusal of all the discouraging information regarding the on-and-off attitude of the military toward accepting responsibility to prepare for the wartime conduct of UW, I noted mention of a conference attended by General Gruenther, Army Deputy of Staff for Plans and Operations, and Gen. J. Lawton Collins, Army Chief of Staff. At the meeting, Collins expressed concern over the status of action taken on a plan and suggested organization for the logistic and operational support of underground movements.

That completed my review of Army actions in the area of UW from the end of World War II to February 1951. The one most significant ray of hope for the establishment of an unconventional warfare capability was contained in General Collins's stated concern since he was the man whose approval for such an organization would have to be sought.

I confided to Russ that plowing through these records of all the efforts to develop military, wartime UW capability indeed had been an ordeal of Sisyphus. Everything had been indecisive, negative, or flawed. It all led nowhere. None of the proposals had sufficient merit. The only redeeming features were the expressed desire to develop such a capability and General Collins's concern. That was all that kept the merry-go-round spinning. But none of the proposals would get the projects accomplished.

Initially, we, too, got caught up in the whirl but, now that the first flurry was over, we could make our thrust for a proven organization ready to function in a wartime situation. Hopefully, enough steam would be generated to propel our proposals off the carousel to a positive conclusion that would end the ordeal.

I suggested that Russ and I compare our field organizational experiences and pool our knowledge. So far, in all the actions I had reviewed, I had not noted anything that approached the practical, tried-and-true organizational and operational concepts initiated and employed in Europe by OSS. I asked Russ to tell me about his Luzon operation.

He gave me a brief outline of his UW campaign. When General MacArthur said, "I shall return," Russ, who was then a captain, echoed, "I shall remain"—with MacArthur's blessing, of course.

On the island of Luzon, Russ initially joined some small guerrilla groups composed of Philippine Army personnel and a few other Americans. From this beginning, he gradually organized a guerrilla force that grew steadily until in the final stages it reached division size (around 15,000 men).

Over the span of three years, this force under the command of Russ (now a colonel) had inflicted thousands of casualties on the Japanese and taken even more prisoners. General Yamashita himself, the Japanese commander in the Philippines, surrendered to the guerrilla force.

General MacArthur honored Russ by having him seated with the senior U.S. commanders at the Baguio formal surrender table.

Then I gave Russ a short overview of my OSS experience in Europe, including the OSS Special Operations branch organizational concept.

We then noted the major differences that required completely diverse concepts. Europe was industrialized, with large, urban centers, advanced road and rail and energy (electrical) systems, and less cover and concealment than the Philippines. But both areas were similar in one important requirement: a supportive population.

"Well, now I have a clearer insight as to what's required in Europe. The way we organized and operated in Luzon wouldn't produce the results OSS obtained," Russ admitted.

"No it would not be appropriate and therefore, in my opinion, we should where possible stress and emphasize employing the OSS heritage," I added.

Although Russ was favorably inclined to the OSS organizational concepts and scope of operations, he had some reservations. His uncertainty, based on his prior experience, was a natural response, but I felt that additional persuasion and future events would swing him over. However, we were on firmer ground in regard to our general objectives.

Russ and I then discussed the entire concept of UW. His

position was that the military must control, direct, and conduct wartime UW operations. However, he was still not sure what type of unit should be organized to carry out such missions, since in a study he had already prepared, he had included Ranger type of activities.

I expressed my reactions to the Army's efforts thus far and we wrote down the most significant items. This would become the outline for our staff strategy with which we expected to win approval for the establishment of the UW force in the Army in peacetime.

We determined the following: (I) Europe, primarily the Soviet satellites, would be the prime target area. Current intelligence confirmed the existence of a huge, dormant resistance/guerrilla potential in that area. (2) Since the Army had never conducted covert UW operations in Europe, the OSS heritage would be utilized as background for all our concepts of operations, organization, plans, studies, briefings, and training outlines. The Jedburgh operation would be used as the classic model. (3) Regardless of the formation of the unit to be organized, its mission would be strictly within the spectrum of UW. (4) To appease the orthodox and the traditionalists in the service—those whose sole interest was in conventional forces (armor, infantry, and artillery)—the unit we'd propose would have to appear, for administrative purposes, to be formed in companies and battalions. (5) We would be low key in our briefings, but at the same time continually emphasize the potential of UW and emphasize the effectiveness proved by OSS in its World War II activities. (6) The proposed force would be only a cadre that would mushroom into a huge guerrilla force, actually a phantom army. (7) It would be the indigenous element of the projected guerrilla force that would conduct UW under the control and direction of the Army UW organization.

By now Russ and I were pretty well in accord on this project. But we were not familiar with General McClure's views on all these points. Neither of us liked the fact that so much terminology was being bandied around concerning behind-the-lines operations. The terms unconventional warfare, clandestine operations, unorthodox warfare, and special operations were being used interchangeably.

Russ told me that in the study he had just circulated to the

Army staff he had avoided using the terms interchangeably and instead consistently used the term Special Forces Operations.

"But initially we will have to define its meaning and explain the components," I added, "or there will be more confusion."

"I'm working on it, but it will take some time to play down all those terms and I'm not so sure we'll ever be without them," Russ said, shaking his head.

I suggested that perhaps it would be more prudent to fall back on unconventional warfare since everyone seemed to know or sense its meaning. To use Special Forces Operations would require an orientation program which was not at all feasible at this stage. The term Special Operations, to me, was the least desirable since it was even more misleading. As it was now interpreted, it included cold-weather operations; mountain warfare; and amphibious, airborne, Ranger, and commando operations. Too damn broad and all inclusive! Evidently, UW was going to be it.

We discussed all the foregoing with General McClure and he agreed with our planned approach, but he was not sure of the type of organization to be used. He leaned toward the Ranger type of unit with which the Army was already somewhat familiar and which Russ was inclined to recommend. In fact, McClure's components of Special Forces Operations included Ranger and commandolike operations and long-range or deep-penetration reconnaissance. Although I had indicated that OSS conducted support activities primarily for resistance/guerrilla groups in Europe with small teams and thirty-man operational groups and that OSS Europe had a main headquarters and maintained operational control through operational bases, the type of unit remained a moot question.

I soon gathered that the reason for this was that in recent copies of memos between General Collins and the G-3, the ideas were Ranger-oriented. Ranger outfits were to conduct all behind-the-lines activities. It didn't seem advisable at this stage to buck the top Army echelon on this score. It was more important at first to get them committed to a program to develop such a capability and then the organizational concepts for such a force could be thrashed out.

In late March, we received a memorandum from General

Taylor, the G-3, indicating that his staff was preparing a study on the use of eastern European refugees, as individuals or in units, to conduct UW and that OCPW should study the possibility of organizing a Ranger company with each platoon of a different nationality. General McClure expressed the opinion that six Ranger companies of aliens, each composed of a different nationality attached at division level, should be considered.

In spite of the orientation on the OSS concept that I had given McClure, he was still groping for a solution that would appeal to him. I felt he was thinking only of the type of unit without considering the command, control, and logistic echelons. Being attached to divisions, each company would wind up performing shallow, behind-the-lines raids and reconnaissance—operations strictly of interest to a division and in no way leading to the conduct of UW and developing guerrilla forces in strategic areas. In short, they'd be Ranger units conducting Ranger missions with personnel especially qualified to conduct UW, particularly guerrilla warfare.

With all this controversy, nothing would be resolved.

But all was not hopeless. There was at least unanimity on the target area being eastern Europe and on the fact that indigenous people would be organized under U.S. control and direction.

Around the latter part of May 1951, we and G-3 prepared studies, in line with McClure's latest thinking, on the utilization of eastern European aliens. The Lodge Bill authorized such aliens to enlist in the U.S. Army with the possibility of obtaining U.S. citizenship after two years of honorable service. Standards of selection were considered and those who volunteered for airborne training and behind-the-lines duty would be accepted for whatever type of unit evolved. A requirement for eight hundred such personnel was established.

Initial plans were to train the aliens in batches of one hundred in a cycle that would encompass basic infantry and Ranger training and then specialized training in guerrilla warfare, sabotage, espionage, escape and evasion, communications, and related subjects. They would then be organized into Ranger companies with a cadre of U.S. trained personnel in each company. There was an alternate proposal to organize them as a provisional unit. In either case, they'd be available to the European theater commander in the event of an outbreak of hostilities.

As can be seen, the proposition was not at all a definite solution, but it made some headway since the manpower pool was a provisional formation and flexible for operations in units of varied strengths depending on the mission. This was akin to the OSS formation in Europe—units tailored to the mission. However, again McClure asked us to disregard the control and logistic aspect. He was now pitching first for the formation of the field units. As he stated, "One thing at a time. Get our foot in on this aspect and the rest will fall into place." This recognition of the OSS influence was very encouraging to me, and Russ became less Ranger inclined.

Shortly thereafter, at McClure's insistence, overriding my objections to the inclusion of Ranger terminology when Ranger operations were being discussed as a Special Forces (SF) function, Russ and I developed a study calling for a SF regiment of three battalions with a personnel strength of around 2500, of whom some 1300 were Lodge Bill personnel. The unit would receive its training in the U.S. and be shipped to the European command in company increments with the mission of exploiting the guerrilla potential in the USSR and its satellites in support of the UW section of the Army war plans. The study was titled "Special Forces Ranger Units." It also visualized a Special Forces Training command in the United States.

Before the study was distributed, we had a final session with McClure, insisting that the time had come to stop trying to sell Special Forces by passing them off as super-Rangers. We pointed out that it definitely showed duplication and overlap. The Special Forces mission should drop any reference to Ranger and commando operations and should define clearly Special Forces Operations (UW) with emphasis on deep penetration (strategic), an unlimited time factor, and exploitation of the guerrilla potential. McClure took the view that the Army was already accustomed to Ranger units and would be more inclined to accept such a new version of a Ranger unit specializing in covert and clandestine behind-the-lines operations. His rationale prevailed, but Russ and I felt that if the study were analyzed closely, it would tend to show that such a Ranger unit could not accomplish the desired results.

Around this time, Col. Wendell Fertig joined our staff as division chief. He had been the organizer of the large guerrilla force on Mindanao in the Philippines. He was also the executive officer of the entire OCPW staff. Therefore, much of his time was spent attending conferences and briefings for all the branches of the staff. Nevertheless, his input proved to be valuable to us in that he kept us advised of the reactions, concepts, opinions, and sentiments of the staffs and agencies with which we were in contact. He kept his finger on the pulse.

# CHAPTER 10

# Riding High

Then, in July 1951, a chain of events occurred that furnished the fuel to propel our efforts to fruition. The Far East commander deactivated his Ranger companies in Korea, where they had been assigned to the divisions of the Eighth Army, to conduct long-range patrols and spearhead attacks—typical Ranger functions—but also to conduct guerrilla warfare. At the same time, the Commander in Chief, Europe (CINCEUR) indicated that he saw no requirement for Rangers in his theater. Both commanders were emphatic in their opinion that Rangers were not capable of conducting guerrilla warfare in their theaters because of racial and language barriers. They were convinced that such activities must be conducted by indigenous personnel who would be trained, armed, controlled, and directed by specialized U.S. personnel.

An additional impetus was furnished by Army Field Forces' (AFF) comments on our study "Special Forces Ranger Units." As I had hoped, it was the signal to cut the Ranger umbilical cord. The AFF's view was that all reference to Rangers should be deleted because Special Forces would be involved in subversive activities. And furthermore, they believed that Special Forces should focus on the utilization of indigenous guerrilla groups rather than U.S.-staffed Ranger units and that Special Forces should be regarded and kept as a separate, distinct organization.

This sudden switch produced a profound impact on us and on the G-3 section. General Taylor, the Army G-3, scheduled a conference to determine the fate of the entire Ranger program. General McClure requested that I accompany him, prepared to present a detailed briefing on all aspects concerning Special Forces.

General Taylor and his staff by now evidently were convinced that Rangers were strictly limited, by their training and lack of language ability, to shallow-penetration patrolling and raiding in just the immediate tactical zone. During the discussion, it became quite clear that this was the consensus of those present. We were particularly gratified at the suggestion that the Ranger Training Command become a department of the infantry school where selected personnel would receive Ranger training and, upon completion, return to their parent units. Ranger units as such would be deactivated.

When General Taylor also appeared to move in that direction, General McClure whispered to me, "Here come the troop spaces we need," to which I nodded affirmatively.

Then the question we were awaiting was posed: "What agency, in time of hostilities, would be capable of conducting deep-penetration operations, including guerrilla warfare?"

General McClure nudged me, "Here's your golden opportunity. Go to it!"

The briefing I presented was naturally a bit lengthy because I covered the SO branch of OSS operations followed by the concept on which Russ and I had worked. But first I advised those present that our term for unconventional warfare was Special Forces Operations. I introduced command, staff, and logistics elements and their functions; the commo setup; and the operations of the field units (Jeds and OG's). The results obtained by OSS were stressed to emphasize the fact that we were not espousing a theory, but exhibiting and illustrating hard, proven facts.

I also emphasized that Special Forces should not be considered as fixed in fifteen-man teams as far as strength, equipment, and logistics support were concerned. They were not to be compared to a Ranger or infantry squad. Each team would be a cadre around which an indigenous guerrilla force of up to fifteen hundred men would develop. This would generate a requirement for support in terms of arms, ammo, demolitions, commo, and other supplies. In other words, a major operation would be organized requiring transportation support by the Air Force and Navy as well. In the final analysis, Special Forces would be behind the development of an indigenous, secret, phantom army, well dispersed initially, but then able to strike repeatedly and disappear deep into the heartland of enemy territory. In essence, what Special Forces would assemble would be equivalent to a massive paramilitary army.

"All this," I said, "would be under the control and direction of Special Forces so that we could be assured of compliance with established plans in the theater of operations involved. And this would be accomplished with a minimum of U.S. military personnel—a good example of economy of manpower! What unit in the entire armed forces of the proposed size for SF possesses such a potential?"

Colonel Eddleman, chief of the G-3 operations branch, who was our main G-3 contact, inquired, "Could Special Forces conduct Ranger activities?"

"As far as reconnaissance and raids, yes, but not raids in force or as a front-line assault force. However, to use Special Forces' highly trained and specialized personnel for that type of activity would be a terrible waste. Furthermore, Special Forces should be a separate theater command, whereas Rangers belong at field army level, available to corps and division commanders," I explained.

Eddleman then probed a touchy spot. "How the devil would you know where to infiltrate your teams? You would not be operational in peacetime so how would you develop contacts within potential enemy areas?"

I answered that we wouldn't drop them in blind, certainly. The CIA was charged with the peacetime function of developing those contacts clandestinely. But I had to admit that, to date, we had no firm handle on getting this information.

At this point I indicated that General McClure had been directly in contact with the CIA on this problem and McClure signaled me that he would take over. He conveyed some of the frustrating aspects of dealing with the CIA and mentioned that the Joint Chiefs were getting into the act.

The discussion continued and finally General Taylor announced that he would recommend that the Ranger units be deactivated. I was elated and General McClure was in high spirits.

Colonel Eddleman came over. "Looks like you'll all be in business before long. Bring over a current study on your concept and a Table of Organization and Equipment. Good luck!"

"Let's shake on that!" I said, jubilantly pumping his hand. I left General McClure who was chatting with General Taylor and sped down the corridors of the puzzle palace (Pentagon) to our shop.

"Why are you so excited and still so silent?" queried Russ. "You look like the cat that swallowed the canary."

I couldn't contain myself any longer. "Looks as though we've made it! General Taylor is recommending the deactivation of the Rangers," I blurted out.

"Thank the Lord!" Russ exclaimed. "Those are the troop spaces we need!"

"Yep! And they're just about the number we had in mind for a Special Forces Group, around two thousand three hundred," I added.

General McClure and Colonel Fertig joined us and, in spite of the mild stimulants available—coffee and cocoa—from one of the corridor snack bars, we had a heady, enthusiastic discussion. We were determined to strike while the iron was hot.

The sudden turn of events sparked by General Taylor's decision convinced McClure and Russ to divorce Special Forces from any connection with Rangers. They now saw eye to eye on this issue.

"From now on, we pitch for an OSS type of organization from top to bottom; from command, control and logistics to field operating units," McClure directed with a sly wink at me. "Sorry it took so long for me to adopt your rationale. But I didn't want to be too aggressive too early in the game," he explained.

"General, while we're on the subject of General Taylor's conference, what can be expected concerning the CIA's position?" I asked him.

"That promises to be a long, drawn-out affair and will be kept on a strict, need-to-know basis," he responded.

"You know, I wrote a study on that awhile back," Russ volunteered. "It offered several options for the transfer of contacts to us. The simplest was, upon the outbreak of hostilities, for the CIA to submit to us the names or code names of their contacts existing in our projected areas of operations, their locations, and all the Intelligence, radio frequencies, and call schedules they've furnished them so far. Another option was an extension of this to include the actual transfer to our shop of the case officers handling these agents. Those not in the military would be awarded civilian ratings.''

That was also, as it happened, McClure's recommendation to the Joint Chiefs.

"And it should be stressed," I added, "that when we take over those agents, to whom we'll drop our teams, direct CIA communications to the agents will cease. All contact then will be between Special Forces Group Headquarters and their teams. The CIA will be completely out of the action.''

Then we went on to discuss another obstacle: the recent stand taken by the Air Force that Special Forces Operations should be assigned to them because the operations would be conducted primarily in strategic areas for which they claim responsibility.

"No danger there," McClure assured us. "The Joint Chiefs are holding to the decision that the Army is the executive agency for those operations. Furthermore, it's been decided that our type of activity is in the classification of ground warfare, a traditional responsibility of the Army.''

"Well, then it's just the CIA protecting their covert shop, what they consider their ivory tower. That's the temporary fly in the ointment," said Russ. "But it's not going to hold us up.''

"I should hope not. Get out the necessary paperwork to clinch the project. Any remaining problems will, I'm certain, be resolved in a workable way," commented McClure.

"OK, Russ," I said. "Let's drag out the heavy artillery. I'll tackle the Table of Organization and Equipment (TO&E) and we'll coordinate a concept of operations. We'll base the whole thing on the operation of the SO branch of OSS.''

Russ was all afire. "Sure thing! It's time to stop marking time. Let's use the term Special Forces Operations exclusively from now on.''

"I'm all for it," I declared. "We're on firm ground now and can employ it independently of any other terminology.''

Russ applied his talents to the production of a thorough, comprehensive, logical, and lucid concept study, hewing close to the outline we had developed, including a revised definition of Special Forces Operations and missions. We deleted any mention of Ranger or commando operations and emphasized the direct action (combat) role of the indigenous forces. Our group controls and directs; they perform the action—covert, clandestine, and overt.

In preparing the TO&E, I developed an initial rough outline for a Special Forces Group consisting of headquarters and headquarters company, including the command and staff echelons and the various support sections: communications and logistics (supply), medical, air liaison, and parachute rigging and packing. Additionally, there was a war-planning section in the S-3 (operation) staff that would convert to a case officer group in time of hostilities for operational control of the field teams. This headquarters would be responsible for commands administration, training, logistics support, and operational control for its operational detachments (teams).

The big question was the size of the operational teams. I would have preferred to set up a manpower pool of trained operatives that could be formed into teams tailored to specific missions. However, to accomplish this flexibility, the Special Forces Group would have to be categorized as a provisional unit, whereas we definitely wanted a permanent outfit with no hint whatsoever of an ad hoc status.

As guidelines, I considered the capabilities and operational record of the only fixed or standard type of formation that we had in OSS. These were the three-man Jedburgh teams and the thirty-man Operational Groups (OG's). The OG's did have a direct-action strike capability that could be used against especially difficult targets, or to conduct guerrilla type of operations in an area either devoid of guerrilla bands or where the force being organized required support to stiffen its morale. From this concept evolved the fifteen-man "A" Detachment team. Combining two "A" teams would produce the equivalent of an Operational Group and splitting one would approach the Jedburgh team. Eventually, the "A" team was reduced to twelve men (two officers and ten enlisted men), commanded by a captain. Of course, the "A" teams were the basic operational units of the organization—the workhorses.

The "B" teams, of which there would be a much smaller number, were composed of three officers and nine enlisted men, commanded by a major. And a minimum number of "C" teams, also with the same complement of men as the "B" team, would be commanded by a lieutenant colonel with a major as executive officer.

For administrative purposes only, and as a sop to the traditionalists, the numerous teams would be formed into companies and battalions. This gave the Special Forces Group a resemblance, albeit distant, to conventional formations. Ten "A" teams would compose a company commanded by the senior captain. Three companies with one "B" team, whose major would be the battalion commander, would compose a battalion. Basically, a group commanded by a colonel would have three administrative battalions. But in the event of hostilities, depending on operational requirements, the number of battalions and attached support units could be augmented. With uncommitted field teams and attached units, Group headquarters would have its operational base well to the rear of a theater of operations.

I developed these teams to carry out the operational concept of organizing and equipping; instructing; and leading, when necessary, extensive resistance/guerrilla forces. The "A" team would be allotted a sector of operations in one of the target countries for the conduct of Special Forces Operations with a view to organizing a well-dispersed guerrilla force of approximately fifteen hundred men. The "B" team would be allocated a much larger sector and would coordinate and assist the activities of a number of "A" teams. And the very limited number of "C" teams would function with the upper indigenous (national and most important regional) echelon of a target country.

All these teams would operate under the control and direction of Group headquarters, which would also furnish all the logistic support through direct radio communication with the individual teams.

Although the TO&E depicted teams of a fixed size, it was intended to be interpreted flexibly so that teams could be either altered in size or combined according to the mission. This was the closest, under regulations governing TO&E's, that I could approach the kind of manpower pool of OSS. It would be workable, and most suitable under the circumstances to our concept of operations.

After completing the initial draft of the TO&E, I reviewed it with Russ and Lt. Col. Waters, a former Merrill's Marauder, who had recently joined our staff. Neither could find any meaningful flaws and felt it should serve our purposes. The only revisions we decided on were of a minor nature.

"OK, Waters, make the necessary revisions and I'll start setting down the equipment requirements. When that is all completed, you'll really have better insight into our type of operation," I said.

"The behind-the-lines operations we conducted against the Japanese in Burma weren't nearly as complicated and complex as Special Forces Operations, but I'm learning," he responded. "We weren't trying to develop a secret army."

I told Russ that the equipment portion of the TO&E would take a bit more time because it would require conferences with some of the supply staffs. "Some of the stuff I'm going to include will not be in their catalogues. Some will have to be obtained from the British and some will have to be ordered from sporting goods and radio manufacturers. The required radios might not be available for some time, like the OSS suitcase radio, and we'll have to use the military model initially," I ventured.

To assure approval of the equipment requirements necessitated briefings of the supply service branches: Ordnance, Quartermaster, and Signal Corps. As expected, they balked over some of the required items. Ordnance objected to the types of grenades (gammon and incendiary) and delay type of fuses and special explosives (that SOE had developed) that had the appearance of horse manure and coal and would have to be obtained from the British. Quartermaster raised objections to rucksacks; provisions for civilian clothing; compact, folding, inflatable air mattresses; stilettos; and escape items such as miniature compasses and files encased in rubber that could be sewn into the hems of uniforms or civilian attire. The Signal Corps staff claimed they'd have quite a bit of research to do for a suitcase radio and to develop the codes we desired.

All this equipment had been used with very positive effects during the Jed operation in France by us, the guerrillas, and the sabotage network.

As the work progressed, I occasionally refined and fine-tuned the organizational part of the TO&E, which strained Waters' patience somewhat.

Russ also refined his concept of operations to be sure that all aspects were based on the Jedburgh operation and operations conducted by the OG groups of OSS. The mission was refined to read in substance: to infiltrate by air, sea, or land deep into enemy-controlled territory and to stay, organize, equip, train, control, and direct the indigenous potential in the conduct of Special Forces Operations. Special Forces Operations were defined as: the organization of resistance movements and operation of their component networks, conduct of guerrilla warfare, field Intelligence gathering, espionage, sabotage, subversion, and escape and evasion activities.

Waters and another lieutenant colonel on his yearly two-week reserve stint completed the organizational half of the TO&E. When the reserve officer left, Lieutenant Colonel Blair, also a former Merrill's Marauder, assisted Waters in completing the equipment portion.

At the same time, General McClure had the Psychological Warfare Branch (PWB) prepare a requirement and a Table of Organization for a Psychological Warfare (Psy War) Center. This was to be a command and training center where Psy War and Special Forces units would be quartered and trained; where policy, doctrine, techniques, and tactics would be developed; and where materiel research and development would be conducted.

The Psy War Center headquarters, which would contain command and staff echelons, including the Psy War and Special Forces schools and the station complement, would consist of approximately three hundred officers and men. This, of course, did not include the unit strengths.

The schools would conduct courses for unit personnel and selected members of the armed forces as well as representatives of friendly nations. They were also charged with the development of training programs, manuals, operational tactics, and doctrine.

We contributed the guidance for the operation of the Special Forces school as it related to curriculum and the development of training programs, tactics, techniques, and doctrine. Although it was taking Russ's and my time while we were absorbed with our priority papers, we wanted to ensure the Special Forces school would start off on firm ground. We realized that Psy War was still the senior element in McClure's shop. This was evidenced by the designation of Psy War Center for the proposed school in spite of our protests.

"That bunch in Psy War is burying Special Forces in the projected center. There's no hint whatsoever that we will exist there," Russ angrily declared.

"We'll supersede those longhairs, you watch," I said. "They'll have a few Psy War units there amounting to perhaps 150 men. Compared to what we hope to have, that'll be peanuts."

Nevertheless, we were determined to defend our stake in the center right from the start. Initially, we felt submerged, like stepchildren.

Finally, we had our studies for G-3 completed. In order at least to obtain the former Ranger troop spaces, we upped our Special Forces requirements to around three thousand two hundred.

"We can use them all, but we'll settle for two thousand three hundred," I said.

"I hope this pile of paper brings home the bacon," Russ remarked with evident feelings of relief at its having been completed.

We were present when Fertig presented our opus to General McClure for his signature.

"You fellows have really gone to town. This is a masterpiece and should produce," he said. "And, by the way, we'll be visiting Army Field Forces (AFF) at Fort Monroe for a conference to discuss our proposed Special Forces Group and Psychological Warfare Center."

At Fort Monroe I was delighted to find a former commander of mine, Col. John Inskeep, the chief of the AFF section concerned with the activities related to the establishment of the Psy War Center and a Special Forces Group. I was not only glad to see him again but also to note that he would be monitoring the conference.

Following my briefing on OSS and the mission, functions, and organization of a SF Group and McClure's briefing on the projected Psy War Center, it was suggested that the center be located at either Camp Pickett or Fort Campbell and that the Psy War department at Fort Riley be moved to the center's new location. McClure objected to the suggested locations but didn't force the issue. However, his objection was noted in the minutes for consideration.

Before leaving, I had a private chat with Colonel Inskeep. His position on the matter carried a lot of weight.

"Johnny, if you feel satisfied with the merit of our proposition, I'd appreciate your help."

"Tell me," he responded, "is all that about the SO branch of OSS on the level?"

"It's all factual, no bullshit at all, and we need your help," I answered persuasively.

"OK! You can count on my support."

"Good! One thing, about the location. Would you object if we send out a survey team to search for what we think would be a location more suitable than those suggested?"

"Not at all," he answered.

On our way back to Washington, I mentioned to McClure my conversation with Inskeep. He was impressed.

"Let's have Blair do a reconnaissance of sites, but make it Fort Bragg if at all possible," said McClure.

In mid-September 1951, in a document to the Army G-3, AFF recommended that a training center should be founded for Psy War and Special Forces. The G-3 concurred and directed that action be undertaken to determine what Army resources were to be allocated to Special Forces. He cautioned that since overseas commanders were reluctant to accept special units within their troop ceiling, emphasis should be on the maximum employment of indigenous personnel and the minimum use of Americans.

Following the disbanding of the Ranger units, this recommendation definitely expressed the sentiment of conventional commanders and staffs regarding elite and special units during periods of budgetary and manpower restraints.

Blair returned from his reconnaissance of various Army posts and recommended, as McClure had wished, Fort Bragg. However, although Bragg was finally approved, the Third

Army initially opposed establishing the center there because conventional units waiting to be activated would have to be settled at less desirable posts. However, everything we required was available at Fort Bragg. It took a bit of behind-the-scenes doing to get it approved, but finally it was, on 4 December 1951.

In early 1952, General McClure sent me to Fort Bragg to select our property in the Smoke Bomb Hill area.

He offered one admonition. "Remember, we have to practice austerity at first. We don't want to appear greedy."

Within that framework, I selected a group of WWII wooden buildings still suitable for barracks, mess halls, adiministrative offices, classrooms, and a library. Rehabilitation costs were only a modest $150,000. A squabble over whose funds were to be used ensued between the Third Army and AFF. With some minor maneuvering, the squabble eventually was resolved.

We now had all the fringe requirements lined up. Still needed were the necessary troop spaces for the center and Special Forces, and the approval of the Army Chief of Staff.

General McClure applied himself vigorously to this task. In January 1952, he already had made a major presentation before the Psychological Strategy Board (PSB) and pursued the question of funds for our proposed project. This was followed, in February, by a memorandum to the G-3 for the early activation of the proposed Special Forces Group for planned actions in Europe and the early establishment of the center in support of Psy War and the SF Group.

The G-3 responded that a review of the reduced budget for the fiscal year 1953 first would have to be digested, but at the same time he gave his stamp of approval to our TO&E and concept of operations and was preparing a summary for the Chief of Staff, recommending approval of the Psy War Center. In early March, Chief of Staff General Collins received the document. It also stated that implementation of the conclusions contained in Russ's initial study, "Army Responsibilities in Respect to Special Forces Operations," previously approved by General Collins, required a Psy War Center which would consolidate Psy War and SF training facilities at a single installation. On 27 March 1952, the Chief of Staff approved the center.

General McClure and Colonel Fertig came to our shop with the news.

"I don't believe it!" Russ exclaimed over and over.

"Neither can I!" I chimed in.

Finally, all our scribbling, reinforced by General McClure's efforts, did bring home the bacon. That was the expression Russ had used and, in my opinion, it was his articulate presentations and capable, dedicated staff work that was responsible for these results.

# CHAPTER 11

# Fort Bragg

A short time later, McClure provided the details of the Army decision to the JCS, indicating 1 May 1952 for the activation of the center at Fort Bragg, North Carolina, with an initial complement of 171 officers and men. This would gradually be increased to 362, although 2220 spaces had been authorized for activation of some small Psy War units and the SF Group. The Group was to be activated in three increments of 600 each starting May 1.

It turned out that the above date was only tentative. Russ started revising his UW European outline war plan. I, with Waters' assistance, developed outlines for school and unit training programs. These included all the subjects in the Jedburgh and OG programs, plus some additions I considered necessary based on my OSS experience. These total programs I was convinced would develop SF personnel to a state of maximum professionalism—superior even to that of their predecessors.

I also prepared a recruiting pamphlet that stipulated the qualifications and standards for volunteering. Basically, these were: a minimum age of twenty-one; rank of sergeant or above; airborne trained or volunteer for jump training; language capability (European) and/or travel experience in Europe; an excellent personnel record; et cetera. All personnel had to volunteer to parachute and operate behind the lines in

184

uniform and/or in civilian attire. For a triple volunteer, language aptitude could replace ability to speak a European language.

The pamphlet was composed specifically to appeal to Lodge Bill personnel, Rangers, and the highly motivated airborne trooper. I did this partly as a matter of conscience in order to make up to the deactivated Rangers. I must stress that it requires some courage to volunteer for duty behind the lines in civvies. Un-uniformed combatants are not entitled to the provisions of the Geneva Conference on POW's and can expect summary execution if captured.

When Russ read the draft of my pamphlet, he concurred. "This ought to get the people we want. You're aiming to give the former Rangers a new home and easing your conscience at the same time."

"As I've indicated before, they'll make excellent SF troopers after absorbing our training and so will the qualified airborne. The only question is, Will it pull in the Lodge Bill element?"

Lieutenant Colonel Blair had been giving orientation lectures on the projected establishment of a SF Group at various Army posts. In late April, Russ started a tour of all the Army service schools and selected installations for the same purpose.

I wondered why McClure had approved the tour at that period. I knew the time was drawing close for the selection of a commander for the projected Special Forces Group. Did that mean that Russ was not under consideration? He had all the necessary qualifications as a veteran in the sphere of UW. If he wasn't to be McClure's choice, then I must be under consideration, since I was a veteran in the conduct of UW in Europe, where the Group was slated for assignment. By happenstance, I was called to McClure's office while pondering this.

When I entered, I felt a vibration that something important concerning me was on his mind.

"Aaron, the center needs to be activated shortly. And following that, the same goes for the new Special Forces Group which will be designated the 10th Group. I took you out of the field when you were serving in a combat role in Korea and now I propose to put you back with troops. You're going to take on the job as temporary center commander and, when relieved by Col. Charles Karlstad, whom I'm trying to snare from the Infantry Center where he's now chief of staff, I'll have orders cut assigning you as activator and commander of the 10th."

"General, I'd like nothing better and I thank you for the assignments. I appreciate your confidence in me. I'll need plenty of help from your level since there is no Army precedent relative to SF. However, I'll miss having Russ readily available in the event of a crisis."

"Just yell if you need help. Russ will be only a short hop away. Nevertheless, I'm sure, with your conventional and unconventional warfare experience, you'll be able to handle any problems in the area of administration, logistics, or operations. Good luck!"

We shook hands and I left McClure's office.

"Sorry you're leaving," said Waters. "With all your WWII OSS experience in Europe, I always figured the old man would give you the Group."

"I'll be by from time to time when I need help and, when you get a chance, come to Bragg after I've started organizing the Group."

I cleared my desk, packed the TO&E and outline training program copies with some of my personal possessions in my briefcase, and took off for home. On arriving at our apartment in Alexandria, I startled my wife Catherine.

"You're early. How come?" she asked.

"I wanted to get the news to you soonest."

"What news?"

"McClure is shipping me off to Fort Bragg to get the Psy War Center started and to assume command of the new SF Group."

"That means another move, doesn't it?"

"Yes. But I'm sure as a unit commander, we'll get good quarters and be comfortable there."

"I've heard that Bragg is quite a nice post, nothing like Camp Campbell was in 1950. And anyway, I'm glad for you. You will be with troops again."

At first, I was concerned that Catherine wouldn't take kindly to moving away from the Washington, D.C. area to a post in North Carolina, so I was quite relieved by her reaction.

Shortly after arriving at Fort Bragg, I activated the Psy War Center with the assistance of some of the Psy War units that had started moving to Fort Bragg earlier in April. A center headquarters was established out of this personnel, augmented by several Special Forces files—Lt. Col. Jack Shannon and Warrant Officer Brunner. This headquarters prepared the center to conduct its function.

There was initial grumbling within the Psy War ranks over the fact that a Special Forces officer was in temporary command of the center. I immediately caught on that the Psy War personnel in units and center headquarters considered themselves the senior element in the center. This attitude, which had seeped down from the Psy War branch of OCPW, would continue until SF blossomed out and, by force of numbers, assumed that role, and later by establishing an outstanding, enviable combat record.

Colonel Karlstad, a lean, energetic organizer and disciplinarian, arrived around the middle of May and assumed command. That relieved me to take in hand the SF volunteers, assigned to the SF school of the center, and start them on developing a school SF curriculum using my outline training programs as a framework.

These volunteers were Rangers, Airborne, and a few former OSS officers. It was the OSS vets who had the professionalism, and they were well assisted by the others. I spent most of my time supervising the curriculum that the vets were preparing, but at the same time I started fleshing out the unit programs in preparation for the activities of the Group.

By early June a handful of the 122 officers and enlisted men to be assigned to the headquarters and headquarters company, 10th Special Forces Group, had arrived. They took over the building that I had selected for Group headquarters, cleaned it, and moved in the office furniture and equipment required to make the headquarters functional. Warrant Officer Brunner, who became Group personnel officer, supervised.

Shortly thereafter, I received my orders to assume command of the 10th Special Forces Group (Abn.), the first such unit ever to be allotted to the regular Army. On 19 June 1952,

I activated the unit and assumed command. Present for duty were seven enlisted men, one warrant officer, and me, making a slim morning report. But it wasn't long before personnel assigned to headquarters and headquarters company started arriving in batches. They were mostly nonvolunteers who had been selected to fill nonoperational, administrative slots. However, the command and staff members were volunteers. They were the first ones arriving since I wanted headquarters company to be functional as soon as possible so that it could perform its mission of furnishing command, supervision, administration, training, supply, and specified organizational maintenance for the about-to-be-organized operational units.

Sprinkled among these initial arrivals were a few former OSS and some Ranger and Airborne officers. These were operational personnel—volunteers. I set them up as a special training staff to develop a unit training program. Among them were Maj. Arthur Suchier and captains Dorsey Anderson, Jack Striegel, and Herbert Brucker. I had known Brucker from OSS China and he had served in my CIC unit in Germany. Capt. Joe Beasley and Buck Nelson, the only West-Pointer present at that time, were also among the early volunteer arrivals.

Using the same system I had initiated in the SF school, this staff fleshed out my outline programs. The programs were divided into an individual and team phase, but much longer than the school curriculum and more in depth, including testing stages. I reserved a later period for the development of a lengthy field maneuver and for off-base, specialized training.

This training staff under Major Suchier, whom I appointed as S-3 (operations and training), conducted all the training for the initial individual training cycle.

I was determined to obtain a level of proficiency equal to or better than the unit's OSS predecessors and at least on a par with the CIA covert operatives. Training in the field of clandestine operations would not be neglected in favor of the more exciting field of overt guerrilla warfare. The whole gamut of unconventional warfare operations would be covered thoroughly.

The chief instructor in clandestine operations was Captain Brucker, who had conducted such operations as an OSS agent in France and later in China. He was a powerhouse—nobody even blinked when he was on the podium or conducted a field exercise.

The period of training for a cycle was lengthy, not only because it was presented in depth, but also because each operative was taught every subject thoroughly. This cross-training gave each trooper the ability to conduct the functions of any other man on his team when team training started. The only specialists that I recognized were the radio operators and the medical aidmen, since their specialized training was on a continuing basis. As an example, the aidmen received their special field training at the Army Medical Center in San Antonio, Texas. This course lasted for some months and gave them a capability never before attempted even for conventional aidmen.

The reason for my insistence on cross-training was that in conducting operations a team would often be split among guerrilla groups, where a SF trooper would be responsible for all the functions conducted by the team—organizing, instructing, equipping, and leading when necessary. He would be on his own, with very infrequent supervision.

That was also the reason for the severe requirements for acceptance in SF.

It was during this preparatory period that the former Rangers and Airborne members of the training staff, working under the OSS vets, gradually discovered how much more complex and complicated SF training was in comparison to what they were used to. They started to realize that there was a vast difference between SF and Rangers and commandos and that SF had a far greater potential. Notwithstanding, it was also apparent that, if required, SF could conduct any type of behind-the-lines operations, the only restriction being the size of the Group. But in the specific SF area of operations, they were the sole unit with that capability.

This was impressed upon them and all the other former Rangers and Airborne personnel a bit later on during the actual training phases. Throughout the training and in maneuvers, I had the training staff stress this difference. I was determined that at no time in any part of our concept or conduct of operations would duplication be detected. The Chief of Staff, General Collins, during one of our Pentagon briefings, had declared that he wasn't deactivating Rangers to have their operations duplicated by SF.

Headquarters and headquarters company was settling down and assuming its role under some very capable officers: Adj. S-1 (personnel) CWO Robert Brunner; S-2 (Intelligence) Lt. Col. George Gormlie; S-3 (operations and training) Maj. Arthur Suchier, assisted by Capt. John Morrison; S-4 (supply and maintenance) Maj. Raymond Doucett, assisted by Maj. Francis Mahan. Lt. Col. Jack Shannon, an OSS veteran and former Jedburgh, initially instructed in the SF school, but shortly thereafter I had him assigned to the 10th, where he functioned as Group executive officer. He was an experienced Airborne officer as well—tall, husky, and competent in handling problems, leaving me fairly free to keep my finger on the pulse of the initial training cycle.

When the volunteers arrived, they were assigned temporarily to teams which were then formed into administrative companies. All were occupied with housekeeping duties; uncrating supplies and equipment; and setting up their barracks, mess halls, company headquarters, supply rooms, dayrooms, storage areas, and a group motor pool. The days ended with road runs, calisthenics, rope climbing, chinning, and pushups.

However, most of the company administration—such as vehicular maintenance, personnel records, administration, and messing—was assumed by Group headquarters, leaving only command functions, weapons storage, and applicable records at the company level. Since there were no facilities large enough for battalion-size messes, we had company messes. But all the mess personnel belonged to headquarters and headquarters company, which also administered each mess hall. Training would be in the hands of Group training committees. Senior team commanders were designated company commanders, using their own teams to assist in whatever minor administrative chores were still required.

To get the outfit into the mold for which I aimed, I impressed all the company CO's with the importance of not only excelling in training but also in all supply and maintenance functions. The point was that although training had top priority, there would be no neglect in the areas of supply, equipment recording, storage, and maintenance.

This eventually paid off when the 10th was judged the top unit in the Third Army area supply, maintenance, and economy competition. A plaque trophy award and a letter of commendation came from the commanding general, a copy of which reached General McClure. His phone call was very gratifying.

"Aaron, this is a bonus I never expected and which has drawn praise from the Army G-3 and Chief of Staff. I've been more than satisfied with the progress the outfit's making in terms of command, organization, and training. But this is something else and so opportune, since it shows the orthodox traditionalists that the 10th can more than hack it with conventional units in administrative and supply discipline. This will serve to deflate their ideas that SF is a free-wheeling outfit."

McClure's letter of commendation followed, which we framed and posted in my office alongside that of the Third Army commander's. In turn, the company commanders received my similar letters with pride in themselves and their units.

During this early period prior to the commencement of the training cycle, I noted in suspicious wonder the sudden appearance of gravel walks and areas around mess halls, company headquarters, and supply storage rooms. The wonder disappeared when good-natured railroad company investigators confidentially informed me that they could no longer tolerate the dwindling of the railroad company's gravel piles. So ended that phase of the beautification effort on the part of the eager beavers involved.

The volunteers continued flowing in, still mainly ex-Rangers and Airborne troopers with a Lodge Bill type now and then. Personnel had been warned to permit only one Lodge Bill man to a team since they would be key personnel.

Major Suchier informed me that the individual training program was ready for final review. This review was conducted by a "murder" board comprised of me, Shannon, Brucker, and a few other OSS vets.

The program covered all aspects of unconventional warfare. In this spectrum were all the subjects in the Jedburgh curriculum: organization of resistance movements and the operation of their component networks; agent training, to include espionage, sabotage (railroad, highway, marine, telecommunication) and power (electric); security; escape and evasion; guerrilla warfare, which in itself is a comprehensive area, including not only organization, tactics, and logistics, but specialized demolitions; codes and radio communication; survival, the Fairbairn method of hand-to-hand combat; and instinctive firing. For a general classification, all the subjects from organization of resistance movements through escape and evasion are covert and therefore clandestine. Usually, the active, operational phase of guerrilla warfare is overt. Additionally, codes and radio communication also fall into the covert category.

In most instances I was satisfied, but since we were under the gun to become operationally ready as soon as feasible, I held back from lengthening this phase beyond three months and did not insist on more in-depth, intensive training. However, after the team training program would be completed, I alerted Suchier to be prepared to lengthen both cycles with more in-depth exposure, particularly in clandestine activities, survival, and methods of training indigenous personnel. Language and area training would remain on the back burner until overseas deployment. However, for the teams with a Lodge Bill man, rudimentary language training would be fitted in, conducted by these valuable aliens. Since there appeared to be no requirement at that period for antiguerrilla operations (counterinsurgency), it was also relegated to the back burner.

With the approval of the program, Major Suchier organized a Group training committee, which was composed of the original training program staff with some augmented personnel who had been trained and indoctrinated by them.

The number of volunteers suddenly started dwindling. The Ranger units had been deactivated and their personnel had been scattered throughout the Army. It now appeared that some commanders with ex-Ranger personnel resented losing such super-infantrymen and tried to dissuade them from applying. If that was unsuccessful, in some instances, their applications were destined to become lost in the administrative shuffle. The same was occurring in some of the Airborne units. Complaints of such treatment were being received in writing by the Special Forces Group personnel officer. Members of the Group who had urged others to volunteer were told the same stories.

I discussed this with Colonel Karlstad and the information was forwarded to OCPW. In response to General McClure's protestations, an Army directive was issued requiring each command to publicize the SF recruiting pamphlet and to assist in the preparation and dispatch of volunteer applications. This remedied the situation and the recruit dribble became, once more, a steady flow.

The unit personnel strength was expanding and we decided that there were sufficient personnel organized to start the first cycle of individual training.

Being a unit without precedence in the Army, I decided it was time to establish the policies, standards, bases for tradition, and goals to which SF would adhere permanently. Briefly, I determined that SF would be a highly competitive unit—truly elite. Just satisfactorily completing SF basic training would not guarantee permanent retention. Everyone continuously would have to live up to our rigorous, demanding standards and requirements. Our standards in general duty requirements would be on a superior, spartan level. In essence, only the most rugged, capable, dedicated, and motivated would remain—the best for our type of operations.

I justified these severe guidelines with the same criteria that established the basis for cross-training: being able to function alone with a guerrilla group when teams were split during the operational phase. This required maturity, expertise, dedication, and leadership, and only the best possessed these essential qualities. Yes! The unit would be the best, with the greatest potential for its size, not only in the Army, but in the entire armed forces.

During the individual training phase, I, Suchier's staff, and selected members of the training committee kept inspecting the training presented by the individual instructors. It was planned that the unit would repeat this phase at intervals. But since we were pitching to be combat ready after the first go-round, due to growing dissidence in Soviet-occupied European satellites, we had to ensure that the maximum amount of training was absorbed.

The first, small, clandestine training exercise conducted by Brucker illustrated the problems involved and the amount of coordination required. For an exercise in making clandestine contact between agents, a drugstore had been selected in neighboring Fayetteville where, dressed in civvies, the trainees, entering at arranged intervals, made contact with another agent. The proprietor of the drugstore noticed these characters coming into the store and hanging around the magazine rack. One would pore over a magazine until another would enter and contact him. There'd be an exchange of words and then they'd leave separately without making a purchase.

A similar exercise was going on at the drugstore phone booth. One trainee would be searching through the phone directory until the other arrived. Here again, after an exchange of words, they'd leave the store separately, making no purchase. Although a phone call was made now and then, it didn't cause the cash register to ring.

The proprietor, not having been alerted to these training exercises, first became suspicious, then alarmed. He called the police, who also had not been advised beforehand. The result was that a few trainees were picked up for questioning.

Brucker was really annoyed.

"Even though I fouled up in coordination, how could those dumb bastards screw up like that and create such an incident?"

"Cheer up! Knowing you, it'll never happen again. Chalk it up to experience and profit by it," I said patting his shoulder. "But above all," I added while trying to suppress my laughter, "tell those apes not to be so penny pinching. Had they bought some magazines or newspapers, that proprietor wouldn't have gotten pissed off and made a fuss."

It took only this one occasion to clue in Brucker. His field exercises were airtight in terms of coordination from then on. He was not the only one to get the message. The entire training committee benefited. Since we would be involving civilians and police agencies in our exercises off-base, a great deal more coordination would be required than was the case with conventional units.

The men were enthusiastic over the program. They were eager to learn and they realized there was plenty to absorb to enable them to qualify as Special Forces troopers. The subjects to master were interesting and different and excited their curiosity, particularly in the clandestine field.

Classroom work was heavily interspersed with field exercises, not only to maintain the exuberant momentum but to gain maximum application and exposure.

In order to obtain the space to conduct these constant, daily exercises, we obtained the use of one of Fort Bragg's satellite training areas, Camp McCall, where all phases of guerrilla tactics and demolitions were taught. Ambushes were the order of the day. Survival exercises were also held, partly in the swampy areas where an abundance of snakes, frogs, and rodents existed on which to feast or rather survive. This one was a toughie—a gruelling challenge that separated the men from the boys.

Some of the pilots of the air wing supporting us heard about this training. They realized its value as a course for downed air crews. They passed on the word. This elicited a query as to whether or not we'd be able to set up a course for pilots at intervals convenient for us. We were happy to oblige. Under Major Mattice, assisted by Brucker and a few others of the training committee, a number of pilots learned to survive, albeit under harrowing conditions and situations—and to exist on unsightly but nutritious "natural foods!"

Among the first batch to go through the course was one of the pilots who had passed the word upstairs. Dirty, caked with mud and appearing completely worn out, he sidled up to Brucker.

"Christ! What a goddamn experience! Had I known, I'd have kept my big, blabbering mouth shut. Torture's the word for it!"

Brucker shrugged. "No pain, no gain!"

As the training progressed, it became evident that the only effective method of truly indoctrinating the men in all the varied subjects, particularly the clandestine aspects, would have to be off-base in a rural, mountainous and/or forested area. This meant selecting one of the many national park areas. However, this, except for planning, would have to wait until not only the individual but also the team training cycles were completed. But it left no doubt that plenty of preliminary coordination would have to be effected, even to selecting civilians who'd volunteer to participate and function in the intelligence and escape and evasion networks and who would permit the use of barns and other outbuildings as safe houses.

We would also ask the local police, state National Guard, and state police to be the enemy (aggressor force).

All the necessary targets, such as bridges; culverts; railroad tracks, trestles, and signal systems; high-tension pylons; and electric transformers, would be available for simulated sabotage and destruction. We'd require large areas in which to scatter our teams who'd have their individual operational sectors with specific targets, where, for each sector, a separate group of three or more teams posing as the indigenous guerrilla potential would be planted in advance for the team to organize into a guerrilla force. Thus, all the teams rotating as the guerrilla potential and then, later during this continuing maneuver, as the operational team would experience both sides of the coin. Unfortunately, this exercise was conducted without the benefit of a language barrier, but, significantly, the operational team would get the drill of organizing, equipping, instructing, and then supervising their guerrillas as they and not the team carried out the operations.

The training went on smoothly and the Special Forces Group continued to expand in strength. In about four or five months, we had not only reached full strength but exceeded it. The team training cycle was underway and tests showed, when the individual cycle ended, that the men as individuals were quite knowledgeable and proficient. The current cycle would mold them as teams.

With the officers and men going through the training together, under the instruction by and supervision of the training committee, they had an opportunity to observe and know one another.

Prior to the initial cycle, to get us started the teams had been formed arbitrarily by the personnel staff for the sake of organization and administration. As the end of the first cycle approached, I set up a committee to discuss with each team leader which men he'd prefer to keep on his team. The leaders realized that a certain number of individuals would be dropped from the Group for failing the course or otherwise being found undesirable. But since we were overstrength, they could be replaced.

Both Shannon and I described to the committee the method the Jeds used by relating the marriage compacts of Milton Hall.

"Since each team will be on its own during operations, the members must be as compatible with one another as possible," I explained.

The result was a certain amount of shifting and dropping of personnel so that the teams could be put on a permanent basis in the interim between the two cycles. Of course, there always would be minor adjustments, but many of the teams remained intact indefinitely.

During the team training, we had a chance really to start observing the team officers and men and judge their potential. I was extremely pleased and satisfied. A number of individuals were outstanding and I had good reason to believe the rest would also blossom. The projected maneuvers, however, would tell the story.

Regardless, a number of the team leaders and their executive officers (two officers per twelve-man team) showed excellent command qualities. This was of extreme importance because, although they were only junior officers, many would be destined under operational conditions to assume a field-grade role in directing and controlling large guerrilla forces that they would generate.

Prior to the completion of the team cycle, a field training section had been organized by the S-3, Major Suchier, under Lt. Col. Bill Ewald, with the objective of planning and supervising an extensive, lengthy, comprehensive maneuver. Among those assisting Ewald were Maj. Jack Striegel; Capt. Dorsey Anderson; Capt. Robert (Buck) Nelson; Capt. Roger Pezzelle; Capt. James McClurkin; Capt. Herbert Brucker, who would be in charge of the preparation and conduct of the clandestine aspects; 1st Lt. Clarence Skoien; and others whose names I don't recall.

The entire maneuver would be based on those conducted by the Jeds in England and later by the Jed teams sent to Algiers, like mine in that locale. Ewald and his crew developed a very suitable plan after making a reconnaissance of the Chattahoochee National Forest in Georgia, where a large area tentatively was selected.

The request to conduct maneuvers there went forward through channels with a request for funds to purchase the civilian attire worn by farmers in that region. I was concerned somewhat about obtaining clothing funds, although the request gave ample justification for the requirement. I only wished there was a way of also requesting the ability to speak the local dialect so the men could blend better into the local population when approached by the region's police elements.

After quite some delay, which worried me no end, we received the answers to our requests. The adjutant, now Maj. Harold Wolfe, brought the document to my office.

"Colonel, here's the response on the maneuver."

"With that smiling face of yours, I assume it's favorable?"

"It sure is! Both of our requests were approved."

I called Suchier. "Art, I've got news on our maneuver requests."

"Don't keep me in suspense. Is it go or no-go?"

"It's go all the way! Bring Bill Ewald and his crew along to the club for the happy hour and we'll celebrate."

The team training cycle was beyond the halfway mark and would be terminating in the early spring. Ewald was directed to establish base headquarters. I had flown over the entire area with Art Suchier and Bill Ewald and we tentatively had selected a base site as well as sector drop zones. They all had been checked out thereafter on the ground by Bill and his "C" team and the rest of the field training section.

The entire staff was also involved in the final planning since we'd be conducting the maneuver for some weeks, with the teams rotating in order to allow all the teams to spend sufficient time in both roles—as indigenous guerrilla potential and operational teams.

The Air Force was very cooperative and an air supply and communications wing was prepared to support us in personnel and supply drops. As I recollect, a liaison officer was assigned to our headquarters for coordination during that period.

We had a resting period at the completion of the team training cycle. Most of the operational personnel were given leave and a chance to rest up and relax and, for some, to blow off steam. The only exception was Ewald's crew, who were getting everything ready for the maneuver.

During this period, I spent some time in the maneuver area and using clandestine cover, clothed as a farm hand, I made contact with a number of the Intelligence net civilians at safe houses and live letter drops. They were all enthusiastic and had been instructed well by our field training section. They understood the maneuver tactical situation.

Hypothetically, their whole region had been overrun and occupied by an invader and they were part of a resistance movement that was being organized and directed by Special Forces who'd been infiltrated (parachuted). They were to supply information on the enemy, represented by a National Guard composite unit including military police, our own enemy details, and the local and state police. The civilians composing the escape and evasion network were equally enthusiastic and had offered their barns and outbuildings as safe houses as well as bicycles for transporting escapees, although most of the underground railway routes were covered on foot. In going through the maneuver area as an escapee, I was introduced to the regional cuisine and the local brew, white lightning, which was just as potent as the Armagnac and eau-de-vie I used to sample in the French Maquis.

Bill introduced me to the police chiefs of several of the communities within the maneuver area. The chiefs understood that whenever any team members or their guerrillas were caught, they'd notify our base and hold them until we picked them up.

One of the chiefs said, "This will liven things up around here. It's been so quiet."

"Well, things will heat up, but I hope they don't boil over," I quipped laughingly.

"If we catch any of your guerrillas, they won't get away," they assured me in their local drawl.

I looked pointedly at Bill and he blinked, cocking an eyebrow. As soon as we were out of earshot, I stopped Bill.

"What made you blink just awhile back?"

"Like you, I'm hoping nobody boils over when captured by those badge-toting guys."

"Our people will be briefed thoroughly on the 'don'ts' and physical resistance is one of them."

"I know. But our guys now are liable to think and react instinctively just like you did as a Jed. I'll see they're doubly warned on that score. Art's going to handle the operational team briefings."

When we reached our jeep, the chiefs drove by, honked, and waved.

"Little do they know how hot things could get!" said Bill.

"Forget it. Your crew and Art's briefings will dampen any explosive tendencies."

Little did we know, however!

An isolation area had been set up in our compound at Fort Bragg where, upon being alerted, a team would be quarantined and briefed on its mission. Then they would be dropped into their operating sector.

The rest period ended and the maneuver was on. Most of the teams, if not functioning as operators or guerrillas, were assisting in the exercise as enemy details, escapees, target guards, and in other roles, always on a rotating basis. This called for very complicated scheduling by Suchier's operations sections as well as Major Doucett's supply section. Both had to coordinate closely with the air liaison officer.

As I told them, "You guys will be humping. Hang tight with Bill's crew."

Art responded, "We've got it taped. No sweat!"

Major Morgan and his communications section had set up a base station at maneuver base to maintain radio contact with the operational teams and with SF Group headquarters at Bragg. The team radio operators and base operators were thereby tested in their proficiency in radio transmission and reception and the use of codes.

The Group staff and I frequently visited the maneuver area to observe the various teams and check on Bill's crew. I was especially concerned with the training conducted by each team for their guerrilla group and how well their group maintained security and carried out their operations against selected targets. Bill and his section maintained a running report for each team on all aspects of the exercise.

One day I noted that Jack Striegel, who was one of Bill's crew and who had a habit of sucking lollipops (jelly beans were not in fashion then) whenever he had a problem, was chomping away on one.

"Hey, Jack, what's bugging you?" I inquired offhandedly.

"Got something you won't like to hear."

"Go ahead!" I encouraged.

"Well, some team members were captured and their teams yanked them out of jail."

A check with the local police confirmed this—with the additional information that a piece of the jail roof had been torn open, windows broken, and window frames and bars ripped out of the separate building in which the trainees had been detained.

Although Bill previously had expressed misgivings on this score, the bird had actually come home to roost. However, I could not deny that the two teams involved had done exactly what my French guerrillas had done, although not always successfully, when any of their people were incarcerated by the Gestapo. Grudgingly, I had to admit that this fait accompli had been an effective one, although proscribed.

Weighing this breach of discipline against the realistic requirements of guerrilla warfare, I closed the incident with the understanding that there'd be no repetition and that the involved teams were to pay for the damage. But the beer to mollify the police was on the maneuver staff. There was no recurrence—the steam had been vented.

The maneuver finally came to a close, followed by an indepth critique. Some of the teams had performed even beyond my expectations. But of course there were others that displayed weaknesses that would require correction. Still, that was the purpose of the exercise. All in all, every one of the team leaders and maneuver staff felt that a lot had been learned that could never have been accomplished within the confines of Fort Bragg.

While the maneuver was in progress, I directed Suchier to make arrangements for supplementary training, again off-base. I had discussed this idea with Suchier on several occasions. Always keeping in mind that we were slated for operations in the European theater, I realized that clandestine amphibious team and resupply infiltrations could be effected in numerous areas. Even though parachute entry would be conducted nocturnally, the safest landing zones in terms of security would be in forests rather than open fields. Since northern Europe and its mountainous areas experienced severe winter conditions, cold-weather training would be required.

"How about underwater training?" Art suggested.

I discarded the idea. "That would be duplication of training. The Navy Seals are qualified in that. I'll get General McClure's staff to check if it would be possible to get a few Seals attached whenever any team requires such specialists for marine sabotage. We'll give them jump training and a quickie in our basics."

After an interval of rest in garrison and getting reacquainted with their families while the bachelors had a fling, the teams, by increments, were shipped off for auxiliary training.

It began with amphibious training at the naval amphibious station at Little Creek, Virginia. These exercises were limited to clandestine coastal landings from and withdrawals to submarines by rubber boats. I went on one of these drills and still remember the delicious food served on board the submarine, which surprised me. In spite of the cramped quarters, the crew didn't appear to be too uncomfortable—a happy, cocky, hardy bunch, the same as our people.

A close relationship sprang up between our teams and the submariners. You could spot which teams had been to Little Creek, since they would sport the submariners' dolphins for which they had exchanged their parachute wings.

Then followed mountain and glacier training at Camp Hale, above Camp Carson, Colorado, and then on to Missoula, Montana, for training in jumping into forests, which was conducted by the smoke jumpers of the National Forest Service. Here the men learned how to lower themselves when they got hung up in trees and to protect the face and groin from being gouged by branches.

Our initial training schedule was completed in the summer of 1953. To cap it all off, we underwent our Army field tests. The staff of the Special Forces school at the Psy War Center administered the tests for the Continental Army Command, since they were the only element knowledgeable in our specialized field.

While we were easing off, we had a most welcome surprise. We were alerted by Russ Volckmann, still with the SO branch of OCPW, that Gen. 'Wild' Bill Donovan, former chief of the OSS, would visit us. It seems he had requested permission to spend a day with us. Donovan had recently returned from Siam (Thailand) where he'd been U.S. ambassador.

I hadn't had phone contact with Russ in a long time, although we'd been corresponding.

"We thought up here that the Group would appreciate his visit since OSS was its predecessor," Russ informed me.

"Hell yes! Nobody in the Group has ever met him. I wonder if he'll remember me by name, or that he once ordered, 'Have Bank get Hitler!' "

"Hell, I wouldn't bank on it. No pun intended!" he kidded.

"We'll have an honor guard out and we'll make him one of our own."

Donovan arrived and, after a day of briefings and demonstrations, he made a very pithy remark that showed he had been impressed by our professionalism—the same that OSS had displayed.

"You have revived precious memories. You are the offspring of OSS. Good luck!"

Donovan realized we had adopted the traditions, heritage, and legacy of the SO branch of OSS.

In the early autumn of 1953, an event occurred that blasted us out of Fort Bragg. There was a sudden revolt in East Germany. Mobs in East Berlin were in the streets battling Soviet tanks bare-fisted.

Needless to say, the revolt was suppressed in typically bloody, Soviet style. But when the shock waves hit the Pentagon, it suddenly dawned on the top echelons that, for the first time, they had a unit, trained and ready, capable of controlling and directing a vast resistance movement.

I figured if they had any confidence in us we soon would be on the way to the European theater. That prompted me to call a staff meeting.

"You've all heard the news about the East Berlin riots. The Pentagon must be well aware that the situation is shaping up as an opportunity to propel us into clandestine action. I don't doubt General McClure and Russ are beating the drums to get us moved overseas so we'd be readily available. Start planning for deployment. Doucett, you and your supply section will be involved most heavily with the packing, crating, and shipping of equipment. Be sure to contact post headquarters Ordnance and Quartermaster sections on current packing and crating instructions, particularly regarding weapons and radios. Limited leaves. Effective immediately, we're on alert status.''

I called Russ and he confirmed that what I'd surmised was being considered. As far as he knew, it was just the selection and availability of a suitable location for us that temporarily was holding up deployment.

This was in line with the concept of operations which Russ and I had developed. Upon the opening of hostilities, or even earlier if directed, Special Forces would have to be infiltrated as soon as possible for very cogent reasons. Initially, the internal security forces within the enemy's satellite areas and its homeland would not be completely in place or up to full strength. Neither would enemy security networks be well established. This would afford increased safety for SF infiltration as well as greater freedom of movement in making clandestine contacts with dissident elements and organizing the area. Also, Special Forces, at this early period, would still have access to the indigenous manpower of military age before full enemy mobilization sucked it up. Otherwise, only boys and old men would be available—sorry material out of which to develop guerrillas.

It wasn't long before the anticipated orders arrived. The SF Group would deploy to Bad Tölz, West Germany. But there was one joker in the orders—a provision that half the unit would remain and be designated the 77th Special Forces Group. Somewhat chagrined, I referred to the biblical Adam.

"Here we go, just like Adam, giving up a rib to create the 77th.''

Thus was born the second Special Forces Group.

Splitting up the unit was a sad event. Everybody wanted to go and, hopefully, get a taste of action. But some would go and others wouldn't. We were all so close by that time, splitting up the men was truly a heart-rending job, a painful ordeal. The split was completed as rapidly as possible because we had to start all our packing and give short leaves to those who now composed the 10th Special Forces Group (Abn.).

Jack Shannon assumed command of the newly activated 77th SF Group (Abn.). Lt. Col. Bill Martin became my executive officer and Maj. Edson Mattice became the assistant executive officer and "C" team leader.

In spite of the precautions we'd taken, a Third Army inspector found that the guidance obtained from the pertinent post headquarters sections was stale and inaccurate.

"Those lousy, goddamn idiots fouled us up," Doucett wailed.

"No use moaning. Just repack on a twenty-four-hour basis," I said calmly enough, though I was seething and I vented my wrath on those responsible over the phone.

After that unhappy hitch, we shipped our equipment and boarded ship at Wilmington, North Carolina, en route to Bremerhaven, West Germany. We were the only unit on board, so the ship wasn't crowded. But the crew didn't appreciate our presence because of all the deck pounding during our daily PT sessions. The night watch had trouble sleeping because of the racket. Nevertheless, to the dismay of the night watch and crew, we did keep in shape.

# CHAPTER 12

# Bad Tölz

We arrived at Bad Tölz in late November and installed ourselves in the sumptuous Flint Kaserne (barracks). Compared to our Fort Bragg WWII quarters, this was deluxe: fully equipped gymnasium; indoor pool; all-electric kitchen; smartly appointed, large mess hall; six-man private rooms for the enlisted men; soccer field; and outdoor track. Bachelor officers had a requisitioned hotel with a club and married officers and men had requisitioned houses. It was a paradise in the heart of the Bavarian Alps.

After getting settled into our quarters, uncrating our equipment and gear, and conducting the myriad housekeeping chores to set up shop, we eased off. The unit got a chance to get acquainted around town or to visit Munich. Many had never been in Germany and for them it was an exciting introduction to new customs and surroundings.

We started getting ready for our second training cycle which would be a combination of individual and team training in our compound and the Bad Tölz valley. This would run well into April. Following that, we'd be ready for maneuvers.

By early spring, Suchier had the field training section out in the Alps selecting training areas, drop zones, and maneuver areas. The area had just the type of terrain best suited for our style of operations. We had decided that the backbone of our training schedule would be a maneuver conducted on a more-or-less-continuing basis with the teams rotating through it in increments. When at base, the teams would continue to conduct team training. The maneuver would be a duplication of the one held in Georgia, but with many more refinements and improvements.

For the indigenous guerrillas, Seventh Army troops would be available instead of using our own personnel. This would be a big improvement, since these conventional troops had no conception of unconventional warfare. This would test the training ability of the teams to a much greater extent than did our stateside maneuvers, although admittedly the language barrier would still be nonexistent. Apart from the foregoing benefit, there would be the experience of controlling and directing the operations of these newly indoctrinated, simulated guerrilla bands.

For the clandestine phases, Herb Brucker, completely fluent in German, contacted and coordinated with the police agencies of the various communities in the maneuver area to act in an enemy capacity. They would furnish intelligence on the activities of the participating teams to our field training members, our own enemy details, and the large Seventh Army composite military police unit also functioning as the enemy. Brucker also enlisted a number of civilians who'd comprise the intelligence and escape and evasion networks and who would offer farm buildings as safe houses. Naturally, these civilians would be working in the interest of the participating teams.

Funds for the purchase of the local type of clothing, including the well-known lederhosen, were obtained from the Seventh Army quartermaster.

Our supporting air wing, which was stationed in England, cooperated enthusiastically. During the maneuver stages, they'd land at the Munich airport, which was about a forty-five-minute drive from Bad Tölz, pick up the teams that had been waiting in quarantine (Joe-house) after their briefing, and drop them on their DZ at night. Then the plane would return to England.

The air wing also supported the teams at base in their drops, resupply, and reception committee exercises. To facilitate coordination, the air wing assigned to our headquarters a liaison officer, Maj. Dick Grant—an exceptionally competent and capable officer who became well-liked and respected by all of us. We would reciprocate by furnishing teams when the air wing underwent periodic testing in their functions as a Special Forces Operations air support wing.

A special language program concentrating on the languages of the target countries was prepared at the Army language school at Oberammergau, not far from our location, where the Passion play is presented every ten years. Teams in increments would rotate for six weeks of instruction in the language of the country for which they were slated operationally. The nationality of the Lodge Bill man, on the teams fortunate enough to have one, determined the language. The other teams that did not have that advantage still had a target country and they had to plug a bit harder in this training to compensate. However, language training for all the teams would continue on base under the supervision of the Lodge Bill personnel.

We were going to be really busy as soon as all the foregoing had been coordinated and kicked off.

Upon our arrival in the European theater, I was shocked to be told that we were under Seventh Army for administration, supply, and training, and under USAREUR (U.S. Army Europe) for operations. Therefore, I had to report in at both headquarters.

When I reported in at the G-3 section at USAREUR in Heidelberg, the G-3 inquired, "Are you a G-3 or a G-2 unit?"

This astounded me, since Russ told me that OCPW had sent over an advance liaison officer to explain our status.

I promptly answered, "We're an outfit that conducts all aspects of unconventional warfare, with emphasis on developing large indigenous guerrilla forces."

"Oh, then you do come under our staff supervision," he concluded.

"Yes, that's correct. Why were you undecided?"

"Because the G-2 (Intelligence) thought you were strictly an Intelligence-gathering outfit."

"I had been warned by OCPW to watch out for and resist any attempt to use us in such fashion," I stated bluntly.

"Don't worry, I'm happy to know that you're a G-3 combat operations type of outfit."

"If you've got about twenty minutes, I'll give you a quickie on our setup and types of missions."

"Shoot!"

I then gave a short briefing, after wondering why the OCPW liaison officer had not succeeded in clarifying our mission. He had appeared impressed with our capabilities and potential, but I could see now that really he knew practically nothing about Special Forces Operations.

We then discussed developing an operational plan for the unit. The G-3 informed me that he'd have one of his staff get in touch with us and handle this.

"Does he have any experience or training in our field?"

"No, but he is an all-around, competent staff officer and with the help of your operational staff it'll work out."

I could see that the G-3 was inclined to have his staff do his job. As a parting shot, I gave him a hint. "You know, General McClure had six lieutenant colonels assigned as my planning staff. They're doing a lot of research on a projected plan right now."

"Well, that'll be helpful if they pass that info to our section."

"How soon can you send your man to my headquarters?"

"Whenever your planners are ready to work with him."

We set up a date and I left.

"Don't forget!" I said to the G-3, "he'll have to know your conventional war plan."

On the way back to Bad Tölz, I pondered this and decided that to avoid compounding the problems of what appeared to be a muddled, uncertain, shaky situation, I'd induce the neophyte staff officer to let my planning staff write our operations plan as far as our missions and operations were concerned. The product actually would be the USAREUR unconventional war plan. All the staff officer would have to do would be to check that the UW plan supported the conventional plan.

Back at base, I briefed Lt. Col. Robert Matter, chief of the plans section. He readily agreed with my tentative solution.

"But you know, our request for maps of our target countries, in the quantity we'd need for the detailed team sectors, can't be filled because the maps don't exist in the theater.

Seventh Army engineers have sent stateside for them," Matter informed me.

"That's a hot one," I responded. "Still, you've got enough for the projected outline plan for USAREUR right now. You know, when your section completes its paperwork, we'll require for operations a hell of a lot of specialized equipment not available in this theater—equipment of which they probably have never even heard.

"Now remember, you fellows have only a brief amount of indoctrination in our type of missions and operations, so don't be ashamed to tap me for guidance. It's just too bad the staff officer's course wasn't ready at the Special Forces school when we left."

"It's a challenge to us," said Matter, "but we'll produce, with your help, the staff and training sections to get us over the rough spots. Since being assigned to this mission, we've studied the training program in detail and have read quite a bit on WWII clandestine operations."

On Matter's staff were several officers who also had served with me on the 187th Airborne Regimental Combat Team in Korea—Lt. Col. Mack Shelley and Lt. Col. Nicholas Willis. Mack had been S-3 and Nick S-4. Lt. Col. George Gormlie, our S-2 at that time, also had been S-2 in the 187th.

When the G-3 staff officer arrived, he was briefed on our organizational setup and on operations. It was evident that he was completely incapable of producing a meaningful, effective plan that would utilize all our capabilities. He, like all the other staff officers who visited us from both his headquarters and that of the Seventh Army, had no lucid idea of how we should be utilized. They considered us to be a super-Ranger/commando outfit rather than the organizers of a huge resistance/guerrilla force: this, in spite of our briefings.

I could sense how insecure the staff officer felt being faced with doing a job for which he was unprepared. I asked him into my office, called in Bob Matter, and ordered coffee. We chatted about irrelevant things to put him at ease and then I broached my proposition.

"Bob is the chief of our planning staff which General McClure had assigned with the major purpose of developing our unconventional war plan and the detailed team plans—a big task and a complicated one."

"Yes, I realize that now and I'll need a devil of a lot of help," he acknowledged.

"Now that plan will be not only ours, but USAREUR's as well, not only for its tactical sector of operations but also its projected strategic one, because we're a deep-penetration outfit as well, in fact mainly so."

This made him even more uncomfortable. I noticed Matter was starting to smile.

"I'll make you a proposition. In the interest of ensuring that a proper plan is completed, our staff will write it for you—the credit will be yours. All you need do is to check that it supports the conventional plan."

The staff officer sighed with relief.

"This is strictly between you, me, and Bob's staff," I added. "Is that satisfactory? It will be a deal, in my opinion, much to everyone's benefit and it must be accomplished in a relatively short period."

"Hell! With the handicaps under which I'd be working and with other ongoing projects, I couldn't do it justice. It's a deal!"

Next, I visited the Seventh Army headquarters in Stuttgart. I was accompanied by Doucett and Morgan. Doucett had a list of special demolitions, grenades, and fuses that would have to be obtained from the British, since they were not in U.S. Ordnance catalogues, as I had learned in the Pentagon while with OCPW. Morgan had a list of clandestine radio and code requirements that were also not catalogued. I conferred with the G-3 while Doucett and Morgan took their lists of requirements to the respective staff sections to explain justification for them. Since we now had our own parachute- and container-packing platoon under Lt. Jim Grossman, Doucett also had a rash of requirements from them, including a parachute-drying tower with a hot-air heater.

The G-3 recently had been advised by his counterpart at USAREUR that we definitely were to be under the G-3's staff control, a positive result of my trip to Heidelberg.

I found that out, just in time at that, when he said, "I was a bit unsure because, just before that, the G-2 indicated your outfit could be put to best use with intelligence gathering and target selection as major missions. In fact, he was making noises about the Group being under his staff control."

"I'm sure glad USAREUR cleared it up for you. Of course you are aware, I'm sure, that operationally we're under them, so that our missions can't be interfered with anyway at the Seventh Army level."

"Of course! But we'll keep an eye on your training and assist you in obtaining your training requirements."

The G-3 proved to be very helpful and became deeply interested in what in his estimation was our off-beat training.

In early 1954, Bill (Bull) Martin, my executive officer, returned stateside to be retired.

I asked him before he left, "Bill, what have you planned to do in the civilian world?"

"Hell," he said in his Georgia accent, "I'll sit on the rocker on my porch with a case of beer and watch the world go by."

"With your paunch, that routine will blow you up altogether," I said grinning. "Anyway, we'll always remember you for jumping with a cigar butt in your mouth."

George Gormlie replaced Bill as SF Group executive. With my schedule, split between checking on the ongoing maneuvers, the team training exercises, and the development of our war plan, the full burden of resolving unit administrative problems fell on George. With the assistance of the very capable Capt. Carl Bergstrom, our new adjutant, George kept a tight ship.

Things were moving smoothly and very satisfactorily in all phases of training. After supplementing the clandestine training with a course in lock picking given by an expert of the Munich police, obtained for us by the Counter Intelligence Corps (CIC) agent attached to the Group, the calm waters became ruffled. The agent had notified Gormlie that the local police informed him that recently there had been a rash of wine-cellar raids in *Gasthaüser* (taverns). Entries had been effected through the medium of lock picking, since no smashed locks were in evidence and no other forms of entry were possible. The police had concluded that, with all the peculiar exercises we were conducting, evidently lock picking was an included subject. Definitely, the finger pointed at us.

A warning was issued that all extracurricular practices in lock picking would be confined to the classroom.

I wondered out loud, "Are our guys really becoming unconventional?"

Gormlie and the agent shrugged their shoulders questioningly. The raids ceased; I didn't have to wonder any longer!

The agent also informed us that whenever a number of teams were on a break after returning from maneuvers, the *Bierstuben* suddenly would sprout a much more sophisticated group of gals than the usual local, plump farmers' daughters. Evidently, the word always reached Munich and not a room would be left for rent. The agent took me around to some of the taverns.

The owners invariably told us, "When your men rent a room, I show them how nicely it's furnished and how well lighted it is for reading. But all they're interested in is a double bed and a firm mattress."

Yes! They worked hard and played harder—typical of the Special Forces breed.

The war plan was progressing at a reasonable pace, but not as fast as I would have liked. After all, we were approaching the combat readiness stage, but being combat ready without an approved, staffed plan with all the logistic support available and in place would be meaningless.

Therefore, the heat was on Bob's staff. Both Bob and Mack Shelley, as well as the other planners, lieutenant colonels Arnold, Heinrich, Willis, Wolfe, and Corl, were frequently closeted with me on complicated problems that stumped them. Finally, it was completed to my satisfaction.

The USAREUR G-3 staff officer was alerted that the plan was ready and that he should be prepared to be at our headquarters for three or four days to be clued in. Then I called the G-3.

"The work seems to be about completed; your man is on his way here to work on the finalization and get final briefings."

"Good show! We want to start staffing it around the General Staff."

"That's one reason I called you. Can you arrange for us to brief the commanding general and the entire staff on this plan prior to your staffing it around? I assure you, it'll receive much more understandable and acceptable treatment. Otherwise, they'll nitpick it to hell."

"Agreed! Call you back on the date."

I got together with Bob and Mack to cook up a thirty-minute briefing supplemented by charts.

By the time our planning section was through with the G-3 planner, the light was beginning to dawn on him. His eyes were opened; he recognized our potential and its vast possibilities.

"Christ!" he said to me prior to taking the finished product to his headquarters. "Nobody in USAREUR had any idea of your concept of operations or what a massive operation this is. It not only supports the conventional plan, but is perhaps the major one for the strategic areas where it can have a paralyzing effect. But there'll be a bit of screaming over the heavy, unanticipated logistic requirements. The staffs have been eyeing the Group in the light of an overstrength, airborne commando/Ranger battalion."

"That's exactly why I have asked your boss to arrange for us to brief your headquarters."

"Now that I'm somewhat knowledgeable, how do you maintain security with all your maneuvers and exercises in the open country?"

"We're sure that the intelligence agencies of unfriendly governments are fully aware of our capabilities. The only factors that will need top security will be the exact location where a team will drop or otherwise be inserted, and when, and that will be available only when a team is isolated prior to taking off," I concluded.

On the appointed day, I briefed the Commanding General and his staff while Bob handled the charts. I stressed our mission, capabilities, and vast potential. I assured them I was not preaching theory. It was all based on accomplishments and experiences of OSS during WWII. OSS had proved that huge resistance/guerrilla movements could be organized in enemy territory where such potential existed. The Jedburgh and related missions in Europe were referred to specifically as models. The plan itself was explained in sufficient detail to demonstrate that, when called upon, we'd also raise a phantom army, since the recent Berlin revolt had confirmed the potential existed.

Before leaving, the G-3 and I talked to the Chief of Staff. He was very encouraging.

214

"You know, in spite of the unexpected and burdensome preparatory and wartime logistic requirements, including a fully stocked and equipped alternative or reserve base located well to the rear of the tactical zone, the commanding general seems to be impressed favorably. However, we'll see what the staff recommendations will be."

"We'll hope for the best until we get the word," I said as we left his office.

The G-3 remarked that, in his opinion, from what the Chief of Staff had said, he thought there was a good chance of approval. "I'll do all I can to push it through," he assured me as we parted.

Shortly thereafter, at the request of General Gruenther, Supreme Allied Commander Europe, Bob and I went to NATO headquarters outside Paris and briefed him. By his questions, I perceived that he clearly understood our capabilities, mission, and potential. Certainly he was impressed because the briefing ran well over the scheduled period which we had timed originally at thirty minutes.

After leaving his office, his aide, a lieutenant colonel whom I had known as a captain in OSS, asked me to wait for him in his office.

When he returned, he was all smiles. "You fellows put on a damn good show. The general remarked that he considered your group as the major operational U.S. unconventional warfare contribution to his combined UW force."

"How about passing on the general's observations to G-3 USAREUR? It will clinch an approval of our UW plan."

He promised to arrange it.

We were in high spirits.

"Bob, we are going to celebrate before taking the train," I said while being driven back from NATO headquarters.

I directed the French driver to deposit us at a well-known restaurant on the Champs Elysées that I used to frequent when traveling abroad years before WWII. We enjoyed a gourmet dinner and sampled a bottle of Château Neuf du Pape.

In our compartment, on our train ride back, we discussed the aide's remarks.

"You know, Bob, if the commander of all Allied forces in Europe can spare forty-five minutes of his valuable time for a briefing on a unit of little more than battalion strength, he must put a lot of store in it.''

"Damn right! And accepting us as the major unit to conduct our type of operations in USAREUR's sector of operations means that our plan, as we presented it to him, will be approved,'' Bob observed.

"Yes!'' I said emphatically. "It looks like it's in the bag! At least we'll assume so.''

"Do we start on our next project now?'' Bob inquired.

"Absolutely! The team plans, in the fullest detail, are now in order. They'll require a lot more time than the one you've just polished off.''

"How well I know!''

It wasn't long after our return that the anticipated call came in. The G-3 informed me that not only was the plan approved but the commanding general had the Chief of Staff put the pressure on to follow up on our logistic requirements.

"Did a call from Paris heat things up?''

"Actually it started a fire!'' commented the G-3. "What makes you ask?''

"Tell you about it sometime!''

Up to this time, I harbored a certain amount of apprehension concerning the permanence of the outfit. All new types of units are considered to be in a temporary, testing status. Since we were the first UW organization ever in the U.S. Army, little understood and with a number of doubting Thomases around, we had been on shifting sand from the start. But the recognition of the unconventional warfare capabilities and vast potential of Special Forces accorded us by the ready acceptance of the Group by the NATO and USAREUR commanders, awarded us the permanence for which I had hoped. Admittedly, Special Forces still had to prove themselves in an operational role. But notwithstanding, the confidence displayed in us by those commanders lifted us out of the mire in which new types of units often founder.

It took some years before Special Forces had the opportunity to prove themselves operationally. But when it occurred in training others and in Vietnam War operations, the SF rose to it eagerly and valiantly, demonstrating the high degree of expertise and professionalism expected of them in their spe-

:ialized field and thus fully justifying the early confidence
placed in them.

There were frequent visitors from USAREUR and the Seventh Army as well as from OCPW. But the most outstanding was the hero of Bastogne, General McAuliffe, recently assigned as Seventh Army commander. With his Airborne background, he already had an affinity for the unit. After the briefing and witnessing demonstrations, he remarked that the Seventh Army had one airborne regiment, but what a huge difference there was in mission and concept of operations!

"The only thing in common is that you both jump."

"He caught on," I thought. Later, General Howze, his Chief of Staff, told me that McAuliffe had remarked after visiting us that we were one of the top, combat-ready units overseas.

The teams all had completed their participation in the maneuver and had finished their second round of field team training. It was time for a break before continuing another batch of exercises. In my opinion, the teams were pretty well tuned up now, as operationally ready as the Jeds or the OG's had been. I didn't want them to go stale or monotony to creep in. No more need for work and no play. In fact, not only the teams but all the staff sections needed to ease up, particularly operations, supply, communications, and most of all the maneuver staff.

The entire exercise also had served to confirm my opinion that we now had a unit rich in leadership, resolve, and dedication and well versed in our specialized operations. Striving to make our exercises as realistic as possible for the next go-round, I had several changes in mind. I brought them to the attention of Suchier and Ewald.

"How about having the teams, after their briefings, flown to England and then dropped in from there? After all, most of the Jeds and other OSS operatives were dropped into France from England."

"It looks feasible, since after dropping a team the planes now fly empty back to their base. They could just as easily pick up a few teams at Munich on the way back," Suchier responded.

Ewald evidenced his support. "I like it! It would be a better drill for both the pilots and our people. The way it works now, it's only a few-minutes flight from Munich to the drop zones. That's too easy for the pilots and our people miss experiencing the long haul required when operational.''

"Since we are all in accord on this, Art, get Dick Grant into the act and we'll see if his fly-boys go along with the idea," I said hopefully.

"Will do! But this could take some time to gel, if ever," Art stated.

"We won't let that affect our schedule, but if approved, we'll be that much ahead," I indicated.

"Now cock your ears for this one! How about German troops instead of Seventh Army personnel as the indigenous guerrillas? Our men then would be faced with the language barrier and unfamiliarity with our weapons and demolitions that would exist when operational."

"Ideal!" said Ewald. "That definitely would test the ability of the teams to instruct, control, and direct foreigners."

"Great! But," added Suchier, "this could be a toughie to arrange compared to your first proposal."

"Bill, apart from the teams with a Lodge Bill man, who all speak German, don't the rest have enough ability in German to handle the training and supervision?" I asked.

"Yes. They're able to deal well enough with the locals who operate in the networks."

"Then wouldn't you say it would be even a better test for them than for the teams with a Lodge Bill man?"

"Yes, it would."

"Let's go for this. Art, get up a request with full justification for this training requirement. I'll alert G-3, the Seventh Army."

The G-3 said he would coordinate with USAREUR but didn't believe the request ever would be approved.

In fact, it was finally denied. Grant's people kept the request for my first proposal under advisement and so that effort remained in limbo.

"Guess we're ahead of our times," I mused.

During the easing-off period, Captain McClurkin, with several other team leaders who were also company commanders, approached me with the idea of raising athletic teams to compete with other battalion-size units.

"I've given it some thought, but I don't want the unit to

become a jockstrap outfit. Being under the gun to be as highly trained and efficient as soon as possible, we don't have the time. But I'm all for intramural competition between the companies during break periods. It will give them something more healthful to do during breaks than hoisting beer steins.

I had been anxious to get the unit ski trained, but hadn't been able yet to fit it in. Since there was a desire expressed now for more athletics, I figured we'd squeeze it in during this period.

The exec, George Gormlie, an experienced skier, had volunteered to organize and conduct such a course. I called him in.

"George, here's your chance to run that ski training."

"I'll hop right to it. We've got a number of excellent skiers as instructors. Special Services will furnish sufficient boots and skis. If time permits, we'll try some snowshoeing."

"Will you run it at Lenggries?"

"Yes. It's close by and has ski slopes and trails."

"We'll put the outfit through in increments. Remember, no schussing, just basics as a preliminary for cross-country skiing. Doc Freeman seems to have plenty of time lately to strum his guitar. Let's keep it that way. I don't want a bunch of cracked ankles."

"No way," laughed George, crossing his fingers.

The outfit finally had reached a level of readiness of which we were all proud. But there were several items that perturbed me. Until now, Special Forces had been wearing an unofficial beret sub-rosa in field exercises, although the practice was discouraged in garrison. I had failed to obtain for the outfit a distinctive, official unit patch or a distinctive official headgear with flash, like a beret. My requests had been turned down.

But almost a decade later, the 10th got a shoulder patch, the Trojan horse flash, and President Kennedy awarded them the beret. With his Irish ancestry, it definitely had to be green.

Following the official issue of the beret, the first such distinctive headgear ever authorized by the Army, coupled with their distinguished service during the Vietnam conflict, the men were acclaimed universally as the Green Berets—a coveted distinction the initial Special Forces did not enjoy. However, in a vicarious way, I later reconciled myself in feeling that I had made a slight contribution by planting the seeds.

219

As 1954 came to a close, I was informed that I would be reassigned to Seventh Army headquarters as chief of plans and operations on the G-3 staff. This was a bit of an unexpected shocker, since I had forgotten about the Seventh Army policy of command rotation.

This would end my direct association with the 10th Group, although not with Special Forces in general. The 10th didn't need me any longer. They were fully trained, completely knowledgeable, and operationally ready. It was time for weaning. They had reached adulthood and could progress on their own.

I felt honored at having been instrumental in delivering the symbolic, flaming torch, lighted by General Donovan in 1941, into the capable, powerful hands of Special Forces, whose generations of Green Berets proudly will carry it forward to immortality.

The odyssey from OSS to Special Forces was completed.

# Epilogue

Having served with the Jedburghs, I may appear to have been somewhat partial and subjective in portraying them as the direct operational predecessors of Special Forces.

Nevertheless, the events presented in this book, in my opinion, reveal that I fully was justified in emphasizing the Jedburghs' major role toward the establishment of that prestigious, elite organization.

In considering the OSS American contribution in this regard, I wish to stress that not only was the input of the American Jeds involved, but also that of all the OSS operational elements.

Those particularly deserving recognition in this connection are the Operational Groups (OG's), the base headquarters, the 101 Detachment, and the lone agents.

The OG's, although having a more direct combat role, also conducted some missions in Europe. The functions and setup of the base headquarters, which directed, controlled, and supported operations, were also of fundamental importance. The influence of the activities conducted in Burma by 101 Detachment furnished a firm foundation for the type of operations conducted by Special Forces in Vietnam and adjacent areas of what was formerly Indochina. And the lone agents contributed considerably in the clandestine aspects of operations.

221

# EPILOGUE

Little was it realized at the time that the combined exploits of all these units and individuals would help furnish the building blocks for the future development of a similar organization.

Hence, it is quite obvious that OSS deserves the distinction as the operational predecessor of Special Forces.

# Glossary

| | |
|---|---|
| AFF | Army Field Forces |
| AGF | Army Ground Forces |
| ARC | Aerial Resupply and Communications (Wings, USAF) |
| BCRA | Bureau Central de Renseignements et Action |
| CIA | Central Intelligence Agency |
| CIC | Counter Intelligence Corps |
| DZ | Drop Zone |
| FANY | First Aid Nursing Yeomanry (Now Women's Transport Service) |
| FTP | Francs-Tireurs Partisans |
| GHQ | General Headquarters |
| HQ | Headquarters |
| JCS | Joint Chiefs of Staff |
| JPWC | Joint Psychological Warfare Committee |
| NSC | National Security Council |
| OCPW | Office of the Chief of Psychological Warfare |
| OG | Operational Group (Command) |
| OG's | Operational Groups (OSS) |
| OPC | Office of Policy Coordination |
| OSS | Office of Strategic Services |
| PIAT | Pioneer Infantry Antitank |

| | |
|---|---|
| PSB | Psychological Strategy Board |
| Psy War | Psychological Warfare |
| SF | Special Forces |
| SI | Special Intelligence |
| SO | Special Operations |
| SOE | Special Operations Executive (Great Britain) |
| SOG | Special Operations Group |
| STO | Service de Travail Obligatoire |
| TO&E | Table of Organization and Equipment |
| USA | United States Army |
| USAREUR | U.S. Army Europe |
| UW | Unconventional Warfare |

# Index